FOLLOW YOUR COMPASS

AND FIND YOUR LIFE'S TRUE DIRECTION

STEVE DONAHUE

CONTENTS

Front matter   v
Acknowledgments   ix

Prologue   1

Introduction   7
1. Leave the Nest   17
2. Follow the Magnetic Attraction   29
3. Find Your Gift   41
4. Make More Mistakes   51
5. Dive Deep   59
6. Return Home   67
   Epilogue   81

Afterword   85
Also by Steve Donahue   89

Follow Your Compass
And Find Your Life's True Direction

By Steve Donahue

Destiny Speaks Inc.
Unit 4, 3341 Mary Anne Crescent
Victoria, BC
V9C 3S7

Destiny Speaks Inc.
Unit 4, 3341 Mary Anne Crescent
Victoria, BC
V9C 3S7
250-592-4145

Turtle Illustrations by Bomi Lee, Book Cover Design by Jacqueline Rimmer, JCR-Studios.com, Copyediting by Laura Moth, Interior Design and Layout by Laura Moth

DEDICATION

This book is dedicated to the memory of my parents,
George and Julie Donahue.

ACKNOWLEDGMENTS

Writing is never as solitary an effort as one might think, especially when one considers the life journey an author experiences before putting his or her stories into a book. I thank my children, Chloé and Spirit, for being the great joys of my life and letting me tell the world through my books what I have learned about life from them. I could not have completed this project without my wife, Maureen McDowell, and her steadfast love and support. She has the keen eye of an editor and the quick wit to make me laugh, both of which I appreciated more than once en route to crafting the final draft. I am also very grateful to my research assistants, Molly McDowell-Powlowski and Rachel Cullen, for their timely and detailed work on sea turtle conservancy.

I am especially grateful for the encouragement from my Korean publisher to pursue and create this book. I also wish to specifically acknowledge my editor, Hye-Young Choi, and the foreign rights department of Gimm-Young Publishers. Readers of my first book, *Shifting Sands*, will know how special the Sahara Desert is to me. I could not have returned to Algeria without the help of Virginie Biarnay, who loves this place and its people perhaps even more than I do. I also want to thank our desert guide, Moulay Harachi, and his team of Tuareg nomads. I would be remiss if I did not mention that the Korean Broadcasting System, by sending its film crew with us, made my journey possible. I gratefully acknowledge the KBS support and the friendship I have developed with Young Joong Jo. Finally, I want to thank my dear friend Peter Campbell of Gumboot Productions. His friendship, and the film we decided to make together, have shepherded me through my own recent life journey that is the foundation for what I have written. This book is a dream that has come true thanks in large part to Peter.

There is a story, always ahead of you.
    Barely existing.
    Only gradually do you attach yourself to it
    and feed it.
    You discover the carapace that will contain and
    test your character.
    You find in this way the path of your life.

— MICHAEL ONDAATJE, THE CAT'S TABLE

PROLOGUE

Visiting south Florida in July has never been on my bucket list. Cheap, off-season rates jam hotels with vacationing families. The oppressive heat and stifling humidity make me long for a Canadian winter – and it's hurricane season. But I go where the work is and found myself in Fort Lauderdale scheduled to speak at a conference for federal law enforcement officers.

I checked into my hotel, ate a quick dinner and hit the beach for a stroll at dusk. To my left was the Atlantic Ocean, where massive cumulous clouds glowed pink on the eastern horizon as the sun was setting over the city to my right. A half moon glowed overhead, competing for attention with the lights from the hotels and condos that lined the shore stretching south in an unbroken, twinkling line for another 30 miles to Miami. Sometimes progress looks pretty at night.

The beach was busy as families and couples enjoyed the cool of the evening. They weaved their way amongst small plots of sand that had been cordoned off by what appeared to be police tape wrapped around small wooden stakes poking out of the ground.

South Florida has at times been a prime entry point for illegal drugs coming into America. Most of that contraband arrives under the cover of darkness on beaches just like the one I was on. There were dozens of these taped off areas and the shocking truth hit me like a punch to my gut – I had walked into a massive crime scene. I

2 | STEVE DONAHUE

wondered what terrible, senseless violence had erupted in this idyllic seaside setting. I began to seethe at the tourists chatting and laughing in this scene of carnage. Perhaps they accepted that a bargain holiday came with some strings attached. I just wanted to get the hell out of there.

For some reason I pressed on with my stroll, which had turned into an angry march. The sunset was over and darkness had chased most of the clueless tourists back to their hotels. I noticed a group of ten people – kids, teens and adults – in a semi-circle bent over and staring at something in the middle of a taped-off crime scene. Perhaps it was a memorial service or some kind of New Age healing experience. I put my head down and kept tromping while I hoped that no one noticed me.

But I had been spotted. A woman in the group of gawkers was waving me over. Out of politeness I approached the silent gathering and joined them. All I could see in the moonlight was the tip of a black stick poking out of the sand. I was right – some kind of weird New Age ritual for families to grieve or shamans to cleanse the crime scenes. Without warning, the stick moved and I jumped back, banging my head into some great big guy that had snuck in behind me. The crowd *ooohed* and *aaahed* in appreciation of the suddenly animate driftwood.

"It's a baby sea turtle – the nest is about to hatch. Won't be long now." The woman who waved me over said. "The first one does all the hard work. Once he's free of the sand the others will be right behind, at least a hundred turtles."

Okay, so I have an overactive imagination. All these crime scenes were sea turtle nests taped off for their protection. Instead of drug runners bringing boats ashore, a female loggerhead, weighing as much as 400 pounds, had dragged her massive body out of the sea under cover of darkness and deposited her eggs in a hole she had dug in the sand with her flippers. Now, two months later, her offspring were about to emerge and make their mad dash into the moonlit surf of the Atlantic Ocean only a few feet away.

We stood in the silent vigil for another 20 minutes. Occasionally, the little turtle, weighing no more than 20 grams, would struggle briefly to free itself and then stop to rest. One flipper emerged from the sand and shortly after a second flipper, and finally it was out and moving very quickly toward the water, where, if he were a male, he would spend the rest of his life.

A second turtle popped right out of the same hole and followed closely behind the first. Five seconds later a circular area of sand about a foot and a half in diameter began to shake and move like a pot of boiling water. Now there were dozens of turtles emerging from the nest. They were everywhere. But something was wrong. All of the turtles, including the first two, who had made an abrupt U-turn, were heading away from the ocean and straight toward the six-lane highway that ran parallel to the beach.

It was a disaster. Even if they didn't make it to the highway, tomorrow morning's scorching tropical sun would finish them off before any of the tourists had drunk their first cup of coffee. The tiny turtles were fanning out, making it harder to keep track of them. We had to act quickly.

We forgot about being tourists and motivational speakers. Now we were turtle shepherds urgently coaxing newborn loggerheads to turn around and head in the right direction. The woman who had waved me over told us not to pick up the turtles and put them in the water. She said they needed to crawl on their own to the ocean to imprint the location of this beach so they could return in 25 or 30 years to mate in the surrounding waters and lay their eggs on this same stretch of sand where they were born.

There were 10 or 11 of us turtle shepherds. That meant we each needed to guide about a dozen turtles to the safety of the sea. I decided to focus on one turtle at a time. I built a wall of sand that blocked my first turtle from crawling to the highway. He was forced to head parallel to the sand wall as I continued building it and slowly turned him back toward the ocean.

The lights of Fort Lauderdale must have been a powerful magnet because he kept trying to mount the obstruction and go toward the highway. Moving diagonally, I finally got my little friend onto the wet sand. Then something good happened. The turtle seemed to understand where he was supposed to go. He gave up on the hotel lights and the highway of certain death and ran headlong toward the surf. Something about the moisture in the sand or the smell of the sea or maybe even the soft sound of the ocean conquered his confusion and he altered his course with conviction.

I stopped building my wall and watched. A wave broke onto the shore and the white foam rose up the long slope of the beach toward my turtle. When the quickly weakening wave reached him he instantly disappeared in the dark water, just vanishing before my eyes. It was like he had never been there, never existed on dry land, like what I had been watching was a dream. I was awestruck. Then I remembered that I had to save another nine or ten of his siblings. I snapped out of my reverie and found the next wandering member of the flock to guide back on course.

One by one we managed to help over 100 turtles find the safety of the sea. I never tired of watching the ocean snatch them like a worried mother whose offspring have briefly wandered away from her protection. When we were unable to find any other turtles, we introduced ourselves and enjoyed the instant bond that arises amongst strangers who've shared a profound interaction with nature.

It was late and slowly people said good-bye and returned to their hotels. I was alone and sat down to think about what had just happened. I have always been fascinated with turtles and tortoises. They are some of the longest-living and most interesting creatures on our planet. Sea turtles have mystified scientists and the public with their uncanny ability to spend decades at sea and then somehow find their way back to the very beach where they were born.

Until recently, very little was understood about where sea turtles traveled for those years and how they found their way back. Now we know that they will journey thousands of miles, navigating their way through the great ocean currents and across open seas, enduring hurricanes and avoiding supertankers and fishing nets. A satellite tag was recently found on a female loggerhead turtle named Adelita. She had been tagged in Japan at a nesting site and tracked for more than 7,000 miles across the Pacific Ocean to feeding grounds off the coast of Baja, Mexico. Some day she will return to lay her eggs on the very same beach where she hatched. And now we know how she does it – sea turtles have a compass in their brains that is sensitive to the Earth's magnetic fields.

Underneath the soft pale light of the moon, gazing out across the Atlantic Ocean, I thought of the baby turtles in the great dark sea. What would they be doing now? Where would they be going? Each one would be on its solitary journey. But some day, those lucky enough to survive would come back.

᪥

I WONDERED what was on the other side of the ocean. Surely it was Africa. In fact, at the exact same latitude on the other side of the Atlantic was the beginning of the world's largest desert. At the age of 20 I had crossed the Sahara on an adventure not unlike what those baby loggerheads now faced. Like these hatchlings, I'd gone off on an odyssey that I had not planned or prepared for but that was somehow necessary for the bigger journey of my life. And, like the turtles, I had made it safely across the great undulating dunes, the sand seas of the Sahara, because I had followed my compass.

People are a lot like sea turtles. We have to leave the safety of our nest and jump headlong into the great ocean of life. Sometimes we get lost, we get distracted, we don't head directly toward our unknown destiny. But if we're lucky, someone or some experience points us in the right direction.

You already have your own built-in navigation system, just like the sea turtle. This book is about helping you discover, trust and follow that inner compass. I cannot tell you exactly where your compass will lead you. The journey itself is always a mystery. But I know that some day it will bring you "home." Not to the town or village where you were born, but home to yourself, your deepest self. Your compass will bring you home again and again to the true path and purpose of your life, to that sense of knowing who you are, why you are here and what direction you must always follow.

INTRODUCTION

Three thousand miles straight down into the middle of our planet, molten iron ore circulates across the Earth's outer core. This flowing river of searing hot liquid metal creates a dynamo effect that produces our planet's magnetic field. We will probably never see what the source of Earth's magnetism looks like. But we know it's there because we can observe its effects when a compass needle points north or a sea turtle navigates home to the beach where it was born.

Inside of you, deep at the core of your being, there is also a hidden power, a force that emanates outwards. We can't see this force. But we can observe and experience its effects. This force seems intent on pushing each individual toward a very specific life. It seems to have its own ideas about who we are and why we are here. This power, deep at the core of your being, is your destiny at work, guiding you to live the life you were meant to live.

Your compass is not your destiny. It's the instrument that responds to the deep and powerful force of your destiny by simply pointing you in a certain direction. Following your compass heading each day, each week, each month, each year, will in the long run result in the truest expression of who you really are. You see, destiny is not a destination. It is a journey, a lifelong journey. And your compass is the guiding force of that journey.

Your inner compass may not begin working within minutes of

birth like it does for a sea turtle. But you don't really need it so early in life. Unlike baby sea turtles, whose mother departs immediately after laying her eggs, most of us enjoy (and occasionally endure) the love and care from our parents for decades before we actually leave our nest. But your compass is always there. You were born with specific talents, characteristics, interests, passions, faults and flaws that aim you toward your very own and very unique life.

Many of us receive a glimpse or even a strong impression of the direction our molten inner core wants to point us at a very early age. For example, I have always been different. Years ago I asked my mother what I was like as a little boy and she sent me this photo. When I was only four years old I was already receiving and responding to the signals from my compass.

At the end of my senior year of high school I was voted "The Most Non-Conformist" in my graduating class. But this created an existential dilemma – should I accept the award? This was a classic catch-22. If I accepted the award, I was conforming. If I didn't, I was denying that I was a non-conformist. In my still developing teenaged brain I felt doomed to lose this carefully nurtured aspect of myself by making the wrong decision. What I didn't understand at the time was that this was my compass. I could not lose it. The only bad thing that could happen would be to stop following it.

But I did follow it. I was a straight-A student in high school but I didn't go to university. Almost everyone is afraid to speak in front of a large audience but I love giving presentations to thousands. My favorite place on Earth is the middle of the world's largest desert. I have always been different.

It's very helpful to remember what we were like in childhood. Directional data arising from our inner core at an early age can be a clear indication to our right life. When we are young, the unusual, audacious or mystical direction of our destiny emerges unfiltered by politeness or practicality. We haven't yet learned that we can't have whatever we want. But even if your childhood offers no clue to your path in life, the good news is that you do not have to create, select or invent your compass. It has always been there. All you need to do is follow it.

REMEMBERING YOUR DESTINY

There is a beautiful Jewish folk tale about an angel that visits each newly conceived child in its mother's womb. For nine months the Angel returns regularly to have the exact same conversation with the child. It goes like this: The angel describes a wonderful destiny that awaits the baby once it is born. Again and again the Angel reminds the infant in utero what its gifts are, what talents it possesses, how it will face adversity and use those inherent characteristics to overcome challenges, make a difference in the world and find happiness as it lives its own unique life.

Without warning everything begins to change. The mother's womb starts contracting and the moment of birth arrives. The Angel visits the baby one last time and offers a few comforting words. And in the split second before the child is born the Angel whispers into the baby's ear, "And now you will forget everything that I have told you!"

My first reaction when I heard this story was: "Thanks, Angel, you've been a lot of help! Maybe you could have gone bowling and had a few beers with your buddies and skipped that final chat we had. At the very least, Angel, you might have just pinned a little note to the umbilical cord with a few basic clues to who I am."

But it has to be this way. If we knew from the minute we were born exactly what our destiny was, life would be hopelessly boring or utterly terrifying – because some of us face truly daunting lives, like Nelson Mandela or Joan of Arc.

I have found similar myths and folk tales in cultures all over the world. The theme is consistent – before we are born we either choose or we are told what our unique purpose in life will be. We learn how we will fulfill our destiny. Then, on the way to being born, something happens and we forget everything. Ancient Greeks believed that the soul passed through the Plain of Forgetfulness. Some African cultures have a tree by the same name with the same result. You could say that this "forgetting" is a part of the human condition.

Trying to literally remember the destiny forgotten at birth is impossible of course. So life becomes a process of piecing together memories, talents, things we are passionate about, key intersections or turning points in life, strange synchronicities and other "clues" to who we are. If you have had the experience of doing something for the first time and it just felt right – like you were meant to do this, it came naturally, you felt deeply fulfilled by doing it or very excited and curious about learning more – this a moment of "remembering." The trick is to then take that "memory" and follow it forward as a compass heading and see where it leads you.

Your inner compass is completely unique. Part of the challenge is understanding the particular way that your own compass communicates with you. How you receive your signals might be unlike the way anyone else receives theirs. Your compass signals can be flat out weird or outrageous. They might be funny, shocking or subtle. And they can change dramatically over the course of your life. As a young man, the things I was passionate about and good at doing were powerful compass headings. In my fifties I found that failure, strangely enough, gave me the clearest sense of direction. But there are some commonalities that we all share when it comes to finding and following our inner guidance system. Here are some things to consider.

HOW YOUR COMPASS WORKS

If you look at an ordinary compass, you will see that it shows only directions – North, South, East and West. These are not destinations to arrive at but headings to guide us. Our inner compass is exactly the same. But directional signals can be hard to interpret because we live in a world that is obsessed with results and predictability. We want to know exactly what our destination is, when we will arrive and what we will achieve by getting there. What's the payoff from pulling those all-nighters at final exams, putting up with assholes at work or resentfully doing what our parents keep telling us to do? Your compass is not a map and it doesn't have the destination clearly marked upon it.

Your inner compass sits in the middle of two mysteries. First, we don't know exactly what destiny the deep and inner force at the core of our being wants of us. Second, we don't know exactly where we will end up by following the signals our compass receives from our center. But there are some very practical reasons to focus on the direction we are heading rather than needing to know the destination.

When I was crossing the Sahara as a young man, I learned that it was impossible to follow a map on the shifting sands of the desert. But my compass could keep me heading in the right direction even if I didn't know where I was. I simply had to keep going south. So your compass can guide you even when you feel lost or confused or find yourself at a crossroads and don't know which way to turn.

Another benefit of direction over destination is that your compass can lead you somewhere that you need to go but probably wouldn't have chosen because of the difficulty or uncertainty of the journey. You might travel through a life experience that is far better for you from the perspective of your destiny. Better because it is more rewarding or more meaningful or challenges you in a way that reveals a hidden talent. It could be a journey that teaches you something you must learn before you can head in a new or better direction.

Woody Allen said, "Confidence is what you have before you understand the problem." Early in my speaking career I took a job leading seminars on how to quit smoking. I had never been a smoker and didn't have a clue how hard it is to quit. I just wanted to give presentations.

People in the throes of nicotine withdrawal are not a pleasant audience. They don't laugh at your jokes. They don't listen to what you say. And they don't do what you tell them to do. All they can think about is how much they want to have a smoke. And since they can't do that, Plan B is to kill the instructor.

So, what was I thinking? In situations like this, it usually turns out that I was thinking just enough of the wrong things to get started on the right path. If I had known exactly what was waiting for me, then I probably would have found something easier to do. But this was my first paid work as a public speaker. It was the only job I could find. I figured I could pull it off. I was supremely confident. But the students weren't fooled – which made them want to kill me even more, and do it slowly.

Six weeks later I was battered and beaten. It was such a brutal experience that I'm surprised I didn't start smoking just to get through it. But the three remaining students from the original 26 graduated as non-smokers. I learned how to deal with an unhappy audience, and in over 1,000 speeches in the last 20 years no audience has been as unhappy as those hapless angry smokers trying to kick the habit.

Most importantly, I learned that the only thing that gave me the legitimacy to talk about a certain subject was my own personal experience. So I decided from that day forward I would only give presentations about something that had actually happened to me. This was a crucial decision that would shape my career as a speaker and writer. And it was my compass, masquerading as naïve confidence, that led me into and through that hellish and essential journey of destiny.

Your compass is about attraction and magnetism. What do you feel *pulled* toward? What *attracts* you? What do you love to do? What makes you feel alive and happy when you do it? What is the thing that you can't stop thinking about or keep feeling drawn toward? The things that you desire and dream of are signals your compass is sending you. Even obsessions or compulsions, which we often hide or try to get rid of, can be viewed as a distortion of your destiny trying to get your attention. But you've missed the subtle messages and it's gotten weird or insistent.

Finally, your compass is about consistency. The needle always points north. Throughout our lives certain themes and patterns are consistent. We keep returning to ideas or images that guide us. Sometimes a desire or dream calls to us but we fail to follow it. Years later it calls to us again. Maybe we fail to heed that call too. But recurring patterns or callings are a sign of a consistent and perhaps insistent compass signal. This book will help you make sense of those headings.

THE DIFFERENCE BETWEEN A COMPASS AND A MAP

In many ways a map is the opposite of a compass because a map is all about the destination. Maps are systems, plans, formulas, reactions or habits that follow a prescribed route, series of steps or specific behaviors in order to achieve a predetermined result. Maps reduce risk and minimize mystery, while a compass points us toward the unknown.

Baking a cake with a recipe or building a backyard deck according to a plan is following a map. For many endeavors you want a proven route to get you to a chosen destination. Nobody likes their lemon pound cake looking like a couple of pounds of Portland cement. Imagine the railing on your brand new backyard deck giving way on the exhausted birthday clown who's downing a beer after entertaining 20 screaming five-year-olds. That would not be part of your plan.

Maps and their hoped for destinations occupy a very big place in our lives. From our personal goals to projects at work – whether we're acquiring a new skill, shopping for a week of groceries, saving for retirement, training for a marathon, searching for a soul mate or picking the perfect puppy at a pet store – most of our waking hours are spent trying to stay on track and get to the predetermined finish line. And that's how it should be.

But that's only half of it. Many of the maps we follow are unconscious. They are the deeply embedded, automatic responses we have for all sorts of situations. When someone cuts you off in traffic, do you get mad and give them the finger? I don't. I just try to pass them and then slow way down just to piss them off. It's an unconscious map. It's automatic. I always respond the same way to that same situation. Probably I learned this map from my dad. And yes, I'm trying to change because I'm a self-help author and it would look bad on my resume if I got arrested for road rage. But the point is important. Everyone has responses to everyday occurrences that are unconscious and automatic. Certain situations and certain people trigger a reaction, usually not a pleasant one, which happens immediately and without thought. We're following an emotional map that was drawn over time and usually began quite a while ago.

We also have unconscious maps about success, work, love, our own potential and our ability to change. Rather than being spontaneous reactions these are templates, belief systems, values and assumptions about almost EVERYTHING. We learned and adopted these maps at a very early age from parents, teachers, family, friends and the larger culture we grew up in.

It's important to understand how much making and following maps is part of being human. Your brain is a mapmaker of the highest quality. Through evolution our brains developed survival responses that we inherit through DNA. These neural maps help us instantly respond to potential danger.

There is a clear benefit to jumping five feet backwards when you see a rattlesnake sunning itself on a hiking trail in Arizona. The split second that it would take to think through the situation and make a thoughtful decision could cost you your life. By reacting instantly to an ancient map in your brain's amygdala the only casualties are the two chipped teeth in the mouth of your hiking buddy who was drinking water when you came upon the rattler.

Following maps is as natural as breathing air. It's literally in our DNA but it's also the culturally dominant approach to success. There's no shortage of life coaches, self-help writers, thought leaders and motivational speakers who will tell you to have clear goals and map out the route to your stated destinations. But you can't map the journey to living your destiny. Following a compass means knowing how and when to NOT follow a map.

DE-EMPHASIZE THE DESTINATION

I once gave a speech about following your compass at a university in South Korea. A student raised his hand to ask a question: "Is your method assured?" His query didn't surprise me because I'm familiar with the obsessively goal-oriented Korean culture. He was looking for a guarantee that he would find a great job, do the kind of work that he loved and be endlessly happy in his personal life if he did what I was suggesting.

I told him that this is not a method. It's a life change that de-emphasizes the destination and places more trust in the deep wisdom inside of you. Your compass is trying to get your attention. Once it does that it will guide you in a unique way that could never be predicted or explained in a methodical system. The only thing I can "assure" anyone of is this: If you find and follow your compass, you will live a life that is probably a lot different from the one you've imagined. You will tend to meet the right people and be presented with the right challenges and the right opportunities at the right time. Left to our own systems we live a more predictable life. When we follow a compass, we live a more meaningful life, although not always an easier one. In the long run, I believe it is a happier life. We grow into our fullest potential, pursue our truest passions, discover our greatest talents and make our biggest impact in the world and in the lives of others.

1

LEAVE THE NEST

There are seven different species of sea turtle and the olive ridley is by far the most abundant. It is also one of the smallest, weighing between 80 and 90 pounds when fully grown. Olive ridleys are famous for possibly the greatest spectacle of animal reproductive behavior on Earth. Tens of thousands, sometimes as many as a hundred thousand female olives come ashore to lay their eggs at the same time. They emerge from the tropical ocean water and swarm an entire beach competing for every inch of sand. Early Spanish explorers in Central America named this stunning display of nature "arribada" – the Spanish word for arrival.

Olive ridley nesting occurs in 32 different countries but industrial fishing practices and local egg poaching have drastically reduced the number of sites where the arribadas occur. You can still see this sensational phenomenon of nature on a few beaches in Mexico, Costa Rica and India.

Scientists are not sure why this turtle and its cousin, the Kemp's ridley, have evolved such spectacular nesting habits. Perhaps the answer lies in the next awe inspiring ridley moment two months hence. When the nests hatch simultaneously, as many as 5 million baby turtles emerge from the sand and scamper to the sea on a stretch of beach only one mile long. The staggering numbers over-whelm and confuse predators, allowing more hatchlings to survive the short but treacherous journey from nest to sea. And they need any advantage they can get. Leaving the nest is the most difficult and often the most dangerous part of a sea turtle's life.

The 100 or so eggs in the average sea turtle nest hatch at the same time. The hatchlings remain in the nest for a couple of days, soaking up what's left of the yolk to provide much needed fuel for the journey ahead. They find themselves buried 10 to 36 inches below the surface of the beach. It can take up to 48 hours for the turtles to dig themselves out of their sandy womb. As the hatchlings crawl from their shells, sand pours into the empty space covering they and they begin to claw their way to the surface. Unable to create a tunnel through the porous material, the turtle siblings travel as a group slowly moving upward. As sand collapses on top of them it creates a new foundation from which to push forward again for another inch or two. They reach the surface together and then the great journey begins with their mad sprint to the sea.

둥지 떠나기

Olive ridley hatchlings (Lepidochelys olivacea)

The next 10 or 20 feet are probably the most dangerous distance these turtles will travel their entire lives. Ghost crabs lurk in shallow holes to leap out and catch unsuspecting hatchlings. Dogs, raccoons, coyotes and feral pigs patrol the beach, alerted by their keen sense of smell that a nest is about to hatch. A tiny twig seems like a massive tree blocking the hatchling's way to the water. Driftwood logs are insurmountable obstacles. Any delay increases the risk from predators and danger of exhaustion. The baby turtles have worked so hard to escape the nest that they have lost 20 percent of their body mass by the time they are on the surface. They need to drink some water very soon or they will die of dehydration. It may be that their thirst, more than anything else, pulls them toward their destiny in the sea.

❧

SEA TURTLES COULD NOT SURVIVE without their nest. It is where they grow up, get strong and prepare for the great journey of their lives. But to stay in the nest too long, to somehow miss whatever it is that calls them to break the shell and climb to the surface, would mean certain death. Simply put, a turtle cannot stay forever in its nest. It will not survive and it will never follow its compass unless it leaves.

We too have nests. A nest is any place, group, ideology or relationship that protects and nurtures us as we grow. Your family, a job, a school, a belief system, a career path, a city or country, a religion, a club or a group of friends are all examples of nests. Our nests are essential for survival. We need the love and care from our parents to get ready for our great journey of life. We need to go to school to train our minds and develop our talents so that we can find work. Our friends and social network are a nest that is essential for our emotional health and support.

But sometimes, so that we can follow our compass and find our destiny, we have to leave a nest. Our compass won't begin to work, to lead us forward until there is a separation from a familiar and important relationship, idea or commitment. The journey that is calling us will not begin until we depart. We need to leave something or a part of something that has nurtured us or provided some important security. This can be a very daunting challenge. Psychologically, leaving any kind of nest can seem as dangerous or difficult as the sea turtle's departure.

The good news is that we can come back to what we have left, just like the turtle does when it returns to lay its eggs. But we come back changed. Something happens when we are out at sea. Following our compass changes us and when we return to the nest that we left, we are different. The other good news is that the departure does not need to be experienced literally. The leaving of the nest that humans do takes place on a psychological level and that can often be accomplished without going anywhere physically.

Without doubt you will leave a nest at some point in your life to follow your compass and discover your destiny. Most likely you'll leave many nests. Some nests are very big, like your family home or a career path. Other nests are smaller, such as a habit, an idea you believe in or a way that you respond to certain situations. Some nests you will never come back to. For others, it will take many decades before your return.

My daughter Chloé had a fascination with horses as a little girl. She played for hours each day with her toy ponies on the floor in our living room. When she was eight years old she had her very first lesson riding a real horse. It was not a pony but a full-sized mare that the instructor placed my little girl upon. I began to wonder if this birthday present was a good idea. Chloé smiled with absolute delight, took the reins in her hand, gave the horse a kick and took off like she was born in a saddle.

When adolescence arrived, she bought surfing magazines and covered every inch of her bedroom walls in pictures of surfers riding monstrous, curling, deep blue waves. Chloé had never been surfing in her life at this point. But when she was 16 years old, I took her with me on a speaking tour to Southern California. We went to the beach near LAX airport. It was the first time she had ever seen a real surfer riding real waves. When I saw her smile, it reminded me of the first time she climbed onto a horse.

During her final year of high school we talked about what universities she would apply to and how to pay for a college education. She didn't have any idea what subjects or possible careers interested her but she had been a good student and I wasn't worried about her lack of direction. I could see that her compass was working. She was able to feel the attraction to do things that she loved like horseback riding and surfing. I knew that she would eventually feel that same magnetic pull toward a specific course of study.

Chloé did have a very clear intention about what schools she wanted to attend. First choice was a university in Montreal. Second choice, Toronto. Her third option was in Nova Scotia. All three were excellent schools. But then I noticed a disturbing commonality among her selections. The respective distances from our home in Victoria, British Columbia, were 2,315 miles, 2,104 miles and a whopping 2,786 miles!

It was fine to be unsure about your career and education path at her age. But attending university simply to get away from your parents seemed like an expensive way to leave the turtle nest. I suggested that she take a year off to go traveling and begin university 12 months later. She jumped at the idea. Chloé was excited about traveling and began to plan her trip, working at two part-time jobs to save money.

On the day of her high school graduation 2,000 parents and family members watched as the students marched into the auditorium and onto the stage and took their seats. I knew that each child had provided the teachers with a couple of sentences describing their plans after graduation. One by one they walked across the stage to receive their diploma as a teacher read into the microphone the short statement about that student's future. When Chloé's name was announced, I started taking photographs as she strode confidently across the stage dressed in the cap and gown. She looked happy and excited to be finished with high school. Her big adventure awaited her. The teacher at the microphone read her words: "Chloé is taking a year off before university to go traveling in Australia and Asia, where she hopes to become a surfer."

But then something happened. It began with the simple three-letter word, "and." Time seemed to stand still and the room was very quiet. "And what?" I asked myself. She's going to Australia. She's going to Asia. She's going to learn how to surf. There's no "and"!

The teacher continued. "Chloé is taking a year off to go traveling in Australia and Asia, where she hopes to become a surfer AND meet her Prince Charming."

My jaw dropped open and I just stared, dumbfounded, at the

stage. There's nothing wrong with wanting to meet the love of your life or just your very first love. What young person doesn't have such a thought? But announcing it to 2,000 people on such a monumental day felt like she had unveiled her destiny.

Chloé left in January with her best friend, Tiko. They planned to return in June to prepare for university, which would begin in September. I received regular e-mails describing their adventure. They went skydiving in New Zealand. They danced through the night at the full moon parties for young backpackers on the coast of Thailand. And they learned to surf in Australia. I am sure that they met plenty of handsome young men but Chloé never mentioned a Prince.

In June I received an e-mail from Chloé. It was time to come home. Tiko was reluctantly returning to Canada. Her parents were insisting that she continue with the original plan and they had already enrolled her at the University of Victoria. But Chloé wanted to stay in Australia. She wanted to spend the money that she had saved for university so that she could continue her travels and continue surfing. And, I assumed, she wanted to keep looking for her Prince.

I never expected such a defining moment as a parent as when my child officially took charge of her own life. She had left the nest. Of course I would still be there to help if she got into trouble. But there was no doubt that Chloé was now following her own compass, freely and clearly. I replied and told her that she was an adult now and it was her life. She could spend her school money any way that she wanted. I told her that I loved her. I felt proud of her and worried about her at the same time. I missed her and wondered when I would see her again. But I knew she would come back. And I knew she would be different.

FOLLOW THE PUSH OR PULL OUT OF THE NEST

Turtles leave the nest when they have outgrown it. They are literally pushed out by their increased size and have no choice but to head for the surface. Once they climb onto the beach a variety of sensory cues pull them toward the water. Between the push and the pull they are able to leave the only home they have ever known. When we leave the nest, similar forces move us to head toward the great mystery of our compass and destiny. You can feel pushed out of your nest because you have outgrown it. Maybe you feel trapped, stuck, stifled and disconnected from your compass and those feelings are pushing you out. Or, you feel attracted to the new journey. You feel pulled toward your compass or the excitement of discovering it and the adventure that awaits you outside the nest.

Think of the two ends of a bar magnet. One end has a pulling or attracting energy and the other has a pushing or repelling force. Your compass can exert one or even both of those forces when it's time to leave a nest. It's clear that my daughter felt the pull, the magnetic force of something she was passionate about, like surfing and the powerful dream of meeting her Prince Charming. These attractions tugged and yanked on her heart until she left the nest. But I am sure that if she had remained in Canada and gone directly to university, she would not have enjoyed it or been able to stay. Eventually she would have been pushed out by her dissatisfaction from not being able to follow what was calling her.

These are the two most common motivations for leaving a nest. If you are feeling a strong push or a strong pull, it's a sign that you need to move. It doesn't necessarily mean now is the right time or that you are ready. But it is important to recognize the urge or longing to depart. These urges, or callings, whether they are a push or a pull, can surprise you and seem to come from nowhere. But they are coming from deep inside the core of who you are. You are being pushed or pulled toward your destiny. You are either attracted to the possibilities of the journey or fed up with being in the nest. Often, you can be both.

It can be difficult to follow these compass signals because we don't know exactly where they will lead us and leaving a nest can feel frightening and dangerous. But staying also has danger. Turtles that don't leave will die. And if we stay in a nest when it's time to leave, we can also suffer a great loss – the loss of our true path in life.

Although the great push and pull of the magnetic force in our compass are the most common energies that move us out of a nest, there are two other motivations to consider. First of all, the nest can disappear. You could go to work one day and discover that your job is gone. Through no fault of your own something happens and suddenly you are outside of the nest.

When a nest disappears without warning, it can be quite a shock. But, in some ways, we have an opportunity that was not previously available. Now we can ask ourselves what it is that we really want. When a nest disappears, it's important to feel the pull – toward a dream or a desire, a way of living that is closer to the truth of who we really are.

Finally, we can become so stuck or trapped in a nest that it becomes like a prison. This can happen because we have been unable to respond to the pushes and pulls of destiny. For whatever reason we simply have had to ignore the natural yearning and opportunities to become free and focused on our passion and purpose in life. In this situation it's important to leave the nest in any way possible. You may not have any push or pull to inspire you because your ability to respond to those callings has been diminished by ignoring them. Therefore, it is very important to focus on achieving a psychological separation from the nest that has trapped you and once that is accomplished your ability to sense and respond to your compass signals will be revived.

LEAVE THE NEST PSYCHOLOGICALLY

Like his older sister, my son, Spirit, decided to travel for a few months when he completed high school. He went to the backpacker parties in Thailand, floated down wild rivers in Laos and learned to surf in Australia. He came back to Canada, entered university and lived like he always had in the same house with me. And he seemed quite content to look for his Princess Charming right there in Victoria. Yet something changed when he was away. He came back different and because of that it felt natural to make some changes in our home.

Spirit moved out of his bedroom upstairs and started living in the basement. He had a large space with its own separate entrance to the backyard. And he came and went as he pleased. He was still in the nest physically, but he had left the nest psychologically.

What really matters for humans leaving the nest is not the physical separation but the psychological uncoupling. Sometimes we require geography to create that psychological departure. But the physical distance alone does not guarantee that we will psychologically leave our nest and find our compass. People can live half a world away from their parents and still follow the family map that was written for them by someone else.

In some African tribes the adolescent boys are "abducted" by uncles and other men of the tribe and taken away from their mothers. Far from the village, in the wild places, the boys stay with the men while being initiated into manhood. When they return to the village, they no longer live with their mothers. They now stay in the men's quarters, just a few feet from the only hut that they had known as home. They are just a few weeks older than when they left that mother's hut. But psychologically they have traveled a great distance. They have left the nest.

If you are certain that you must leave a nest, consider what is required to accomplish the psychological departure. It is possible that a single symbolic ritual can create the required separation. Or, you might have a daily ritual that accomplishes the same separation and frees you to find, follow, or at the very least feel connected to your inner compass.

The wisdom of your inner core, that mysterious source of your destiny, wants something good to happen for you. But it also knows that for the journey to begin or continue, for a rebirth to occur, there are times that we have to make a break, a separation. And since the separation must be complete and thorough and real on a psychological level, the way it unfolds in our life can feel very frightening indeed. It can feel like death, like loss at the deepest level. When those adolescent African boys are taken away for initiation into manhood, their mothers hold a funeral for them. Their boys have "died." When the son comes back in a few weeks, he is no longer a child. He is a man.

Finally, a departure can be complete and psychological by being specific. We can be very selective about exactly what we are leaving. For example, you might not leave school but just change your course of study. You might not leave the company but find a different job within it. You might not leave your marriage but stop a certain way of acting or thinking that has contributed to the difficulties.

TIMING IS EVERYTHING

Timing is crucial when it comes to nest departures. Turtles that leave their nest in daylight face much greater danger making it to the sea than those who hatch at night. The sand can be so hot on tropical beaches that they perish before reaching the water. Birds of prey swoop down from the sky and pluck the hatchlings from the sand and the surf.

For humans, unfortunately, it's very hard to give generalized advice about timing. There are risks with leaving too soon as well as too late. I know people who've waited too long and it became harder and harder to leave the more they waited. I know others who were too eager, left too soon and suffered greatly from not being ready.

So how do you know when to leave a nest? The simple answer is to leave when you are ready. Something deep inside you says, "It's time!" Nests are a place of incubation. You should be growing, learning and getting stronger in the nest. The nest is a place of security and safety. So if the nest becomes unsafe and you can no longer grow, then it is time to go.

The big mistake is that people leave nests just because they become uncomfortable. Often, discomfort in a nest is a sign that you have an opportunity to learn and grow. By dealing with the problem or difficult situation we tap into our deeper resources and are forced to change in order to stay in the nest. It's important when a nest becomes uncomfortable to determine whether or not you can continue to grow in it. Perhaps you can find a way to make the nest more secure and more supportive by facing the situation and learning from it rather than leaving.

I don't want you to become a gypsy wandering from job to job, country to country, marriage to marriage because you keep feeling uncomfortable in the nest. That is simply running away whenever you are uncomfortable. Paradoxically, the more you have contact with your compass, the more you will actually be able to stay when things are uncomfortable. Because your life has deeper meaning and because the compass leads you on the journey that can't be mapped out you will always be having new experiences, new challenges and new successes even though you didn't physically go anywhere. But sometimes you have to go. You are getting pushed out of the the nest. You have outgrown it and the nest is no longer safe and secure. Staying becomes dangerous.

So leave when you are ready. When it feels right. Or, leave when you have a sign. Sometimes we have synchronistic experiences that confirm what we have been feeling inside. We meet someone or have a series of experiences that are unusual or out of the ordinary and can only be explained as a signal that we're ready. An opportunity may present itself such as a job offer, a chance to study abroad or a project to work on. The timing is right. You can't pass up this opportunity.

Do not confuse "being ready" with "being prepared." The problem with moving away from security and toward destiny is that we really don't know what to expect and it would be impossible to be completely prepared. Of course, it makes sense to do obvious and necessary things to prepare as best you can. But, the "being ready" that I'm referring to is about a feeling inside of you that just says "now is the time."

There is no map for nest departures. We are completely under the sway of forces deep inside of us when it comes to the moment of leaving. As soon as we leave, a new world opens up and our compass begins to function and point us in the direction of destiny.

2

FOLLOW THE MAGNETIC ATTRACTION

Scientific research on sea turtle navigation began with the work of Archie Carr in the 1940s and 1950s. Carr was a naturalist and professor of zoology at the University of Florida, where he taught for most of his life. He is known as the "father of sea turtle research" and is widely credited with helping save a number of sea turtle species from extinction in the 20th century.

Carr focused many of his efforts on halting the precipitous decline in the green turtle population. A large and beautiful animal, a green turtle can weigh over 400 pounds. It has an attractive, inquisitive face and swims effortlessly with powerful strokes from its front flippers. Green turtles are also very tasty. They are still hunted for their meat. Hopefully, countries around the world will protect this elegant creature so that its numbers stop declining and the species will survive.

Ironically, it is thanks to turtle hunters that we first began to understand the sea turtle's magnificent ability to navigate the open seas. Green turtles have always been a favorite of turtle hunters because they are very docile, which makes it easier to transport them long distances, and they can remain alive for months in captivity. In the first half of the 20th century, Caribbean fishermen would carve their initials into the underside of the turtle's shell so that each boat would be paid correctly for its particular catch. Then the animals would be transferred to a larger boat heading to the market in Florida.

In his book *The Windward Road*, published in 1956, Archie Carr recounts the story of turtle fisherman who had caught and branded a number of green turtles at their feeding grounds off the coast of Nicaragua. Carr describes how the transfer vessel laden with these particular turtles was caught in a terrible storm in the Gulf of Mexico as it neared its destination of Key West, Florida. The boat sank and the green turtles escaped. But their good luck wouldn't last. Two months later a couple of the branded turtles were recaptured by the same fishermen in the exact same feeding grounds near Nicaragua. They had found their way back across 600 miles of unfamiliar water.

Although an accidental experiment, the return of the branded turtles proved that they had an innate ability to navigate toward a specific destination. And thus began the quest to identify the source of their directional prowess. In the end, it was a very simple experiment that finally exposed the secret of the sea turtle's uncanny seamanship. Scientists placed hatchlings in a circular vat of water and controlled the geomagnetic field. By altering the field they could change the direction that the turtles would swim. We now know that sea turtles have a functioning compass at birth. But other studies have shown that the precision of a turtle's compass increases with age. Young turtles are able to navigate generally within large ocean regions. As they become older they can locate specific feeding grounds. Finally, as fully mature adults, they are able to return to the exact location of the beach where they were born by simply responding to the magnetic attraction that they feel.

🐢

LOCATE YOUR COMPASS

A sea turtle's compass is located in its head. Magnetite, a form of iron with magnetic properties, is found in high concentrations in even a newborn hatchling's brain. As soon as it enters the water the turtle can begin orienting itself magnetically. Turtles seem to remember the magnetic signature of everywhere they travel, which enables them to return to feeding grounds and nesting sites. Their head is like the magnetized needle of a real compass pointing them in the direction they need to go.

Green sea turtle (Chelonia mydas)

To better follow our compass we should consider the "location" of our uniquely human version of this "organ." Think of it as residing in your heart rather than your head. The heart is a better "location" because compass signals often resemble feelings more than thoughts. Compass directions don't always make sense but they usually move us emotionally.

The heart symbolizes love – the people that we love, the things that we love to do, the way that we find love in the world and allow ourselves to be loved are clues to the direction that our compass is pointing. To follow our compass is maybe the highest form of loving ourselves. Like love, the compass is hard to figure out at times. Finally, to lose our compass heading, or to know it but not be able to follow it, can feel like your heart has been broken.

This chapter is about following your heart, listening to your heart, cultivating a relationship with your heart. It's about responding to attractions, passions, desires and dreams while developing the sensitivity to discern your genuine heart-centered compass signals from the multitude of everyday urges. By learning to feel what your deep heart wants, you can make decisions based on your compass signals rather than relying exclusively on maps and thoughts in your head.

Here is an exercise that I used to show my ballroom dancing students. Stand tall against a wall with your heels, buttocks, upper back and head making contact with the wall. Pull your stomach in, lift your chest and relax your shoulders. Feel your head balance lightly, almost floating on top of your spine as it stays in contact with the wall. You should be in a position of perfect posture. Now step away from the wall. What part of you moved first? Your feet? Certainly not. When you have perfectly balanced posture, it will be your chest that begins a walking movement. In other words, your heart literally is leading you forward.

Try to walk in this balanced position a little bit each day. Move the focus of your awareness from your head down into your heart. Rather than thinking about everything, try feeling from your heart where you should go. Notice what attracts you and go toward it if you can. If you can't take the time to do this walking exercise, just place your hand over your heart, take a deep breath and try to feel what your heart wants. This simple practice can help you locate the signals coming from your deep inner core. Then, like the turtle, your compass can start to lead the way.

When we are around two years old, we begin to identify what we want and make verbal demands on our parents. We call this developmental stage the "terrible twos." This can be a trying time for both parents and child as the young person starts to learn that it cannot have everything that it wants when it wants it. It can drive a parent completely crazy but it is a necessary and unavoidable experience for growing up. It is also the beginning of losing touch with the purity of wanting what we want. We learn that many of the things we want cannot be had and the yearning, desires and passions we feel are not to be trusted or pursued. In fact, those feelings can get us into a lot of trouble.

I don't want to over-romanticize the importance of pursuing what we are attracted to. When it comes to following the magnetic attraction of our compass, we have to be prepared for a few bumps in the road. The trick is to get into the right kind of trouble. Sometimes our attractions lead us into the precise predicaments that help us grow and learn and mature so that we become more capable of following the real direction of our lives.

When I was a boy, I loved to go to the movies with my five sisters and my little brother. There was a rundown cinema at the Toledo Zoo that showed older movies and Sunday afternoon was the family matinee. "Family" of course meant "kids," for I never saw an adult of any sort brave or foolish enough to enter the theater during that time. Parents would drive up and open the car doors, the kids would pour out and run into the cinema and total bedlam would break out. We would get into a lot of trouble at the Sunday afternoon movie.

As soon as the lights would go out, all the boys would take their slingshots and shoot small hard candies purchased from the concession stand at the silver screen. Girls would yell at us to stop so that they could watch the movie but they didn't watch the movie. They talked loudly and giggled and kept jumping up and running to another seat to talk to a different friend. Eventually a teenaged usher in a red tuxedo jacket and black bow tie carrying only a flashlight would enter the theater in a feeble attempt to restore peace to what was quickly becoming a mass riot.

Getting caught by the usher for any misbehavior meant that you would be in trouble, big trouble. You would be evicted from the theater, your parents would be phoned and they would have to come early to pick you up or you would have to wait outside until the film was over. But there would be punishment, banishment next week or for several weeks from the very place of joy and mayhem and trouble, the Sunday afternoon matinee.

When the movie finished, we would stagger out of the darkness shielding our eyes from the harsh light of real life outside. Our stomachs were bloated with junk food, our feet were sticking to the pavement from the spilled soft drinks we'd stepped in, but we were happy having spent a couple of hours completely free of our parents' control while being utterly wild and doing what we loved. The parent who picked us up would always ask, "How was the movie?" and I always replied, "It was fine," hoping that was they didn't need details because I doubt there was more than one movie in all those years that I actually watched. But one was enough.

At the 1962 Academy Awards, *Lawrence of Arabia* won seven Oscars. Peter O'Toole, an Irish stage actor in his first major film role, portrayed the enigmatic British Army officer T.E. Lawrence, who led the Arab revolt against the Turkish Ottoman Empire during the First World War. I was nine or ten years old when I first saw this magnificent movie as a rerun at our bedraggled cinema.

The film attempted to capture the complex, conflicted personality of the real-life T.E. Lawrence. But those subtleties were missed by the wide-eyed, awestruck and hero-worshipping child that I was. All I saw was a handsome, courageous soldier garbed in exotic desert robes racing over endless dunes on a white fighting camel with his saber drawn. I'm sure the tattered Toledo Zoo theater this particular Sunday afternoon was in its usual state of complete juvenile anarchy. But I don't remember being disturbed by my friends firing their slingshots or the girls gabbing constantly. I was utterly transfixed by the desert images, battle scenes and this dashing English officer dressed like a nomadic warrior. When the film finished, everyone bolted for the exit. I stayed in my seat, stuck in a dream and unable to move, and stared at the credits rolling past as the stirring soundtrack with its haunting Middle Eastern melodies played to its conclusion. When I finally emerged from the theater into the blinding summer glare, I suddenly became Lawrence of Arabia in the midday sun of a faraway desert land. My parents' car was a British general's vehicle fetching me from the campaign to return to Cairo, where I would plan our next daring attack. My brother and sisters were potential Turkish spies, so when my father asked how the movie was, I said absolutely nothing. Inside my heart, one of the great magnetic attractions of my life had begun to pull me toward my destiny.

For the next few weeks the wooded ravine behind my house became the great sands of Arabia. My little brother, Dan, and cousin Andy were my Bedouin lieutenants as we fought our Turkish oppressors and drove them from our cherished desert home. The soft mud along the banks of the slow-flowing Delaware Creek was imaginary quicksand and my dog Star a fearless fighting camel leading the charge in every battle. The boyhood games played on imaginary deserts faded away as I grew up. But the images of an endless desert and nomadic people wrapped from head to toe in flowing garments were seared into my soul. Ten years later I was a young man backpacking and hitchhiking through Europe. A chance encounter led to an opportunity to cross the Sahara Desert. It was a risky endeavor with gaps in the planning and any reasonable assessment of the adventure would have made me run in the other direction. But the magnetic attraction entranced me and within weeks I found myself in the middle of the world's largest desert experiencing no end of trouble as I described in my first book, *Shifting Sands*.

Lawrence's desert on the Arabian Peninsula was replaced by North Africa's Sahara. Bedouin tribesmen became Tuareg nomads. I never tried soldiering but I turned my Saharan experiences into a career as a motivational speaker and a book that became a bestseller. I've traveled the world telling the story of that epic journey. I've even made a documentary film about my emotional return to Algeria 33 years later. I remain utterly fascinated with the image of a sea of sand stretching to the horizon and a man in a blue turban and flowing robes on a white camel racing over the dunes. This compass heading continues to shape the story of my life and I doubt that will ever change.

PRACTICE MAKES PERFECT

Like with sea turtles, the accuracy of your compass improves with practice. Give yourself permission to do more of the things that you love. Don't focus on achieving anything special from following an attraction. Do it as a form of practice. This tells your heart that you are listening to it.

If there is something that you've been wanting to do for a while – an activity, a hobby, trying a type of food that you're interested in – follow that attraction. If there is a kind of music that interests you, find out everything you can about it and go to the clubs where it is played. If you're attracted to a certain culture or country, try to go there. Learn to speak that language. Follow that attraction and see where it takes you.

Make note of what attracts you. At the end of the day, look at your list and count how many things caught the attention of your heart. Do it again the next day or perhaps a week later and see if the list increased in length. See if the same kinds of things attracted you. Just noticing what attracts you will increase your sensitivity to the magnetic pull of your compass.

Keeping track of your attractions over a period of time will help you notice patterns. Recurring themes in your attractions can be very influential for directing the course of your life. As with the distinct magnetic signature of each location that a sea turtle responds to, we are also drawn toward very specific and thematically similar things. If a certain type of attraction keeps showing up on your list, even in different forms or different situations, then you may be getting a glimpse at one of the big compass headings of your life.

Sometimes attractions lead nowhere. What really matters is that you followed the attraction and by doing so you increased your ability to sense your compass signals. Your heart begins to trust you. The more that your heart trusts you, the better your chances that it will reveal its secrets and lead you deeper into your true self and true purpose, and toward the true path for your journey in life.

FOLLOW ONE ATTRACTION TO THE NEXT

Baby green turtles begin life attracted to a variety of food sources. They eat almost anything they come across. But eventually they find their way toward the most consistent and powerful attraction in their lives: sea grass. Once they reach a certain age, green turtles will consume almost nothing else. They are the only sea turtle species that develops a primarily herbivore diet. If you are ever vacationing in the tropics and are lucky enough to spot a turtle nibbling the short green leaves growing out of the seabed, then you have seen one of the most magnificent creatures of the ocean. Its steady diet of grass gives this turtle its distinctive color, its name and unfortunately, its flavor. But without this single dominating attraction the green turtle could not live its destiny.

We are trying to get to the really powerful forces of your personal destiny. Somewhere inside of you, at that molten core in the center of your being, is the really big attraction of your life. It is your sea grass. The thing you are attracted to that will feed you and make you who you are. Maybe for humans, there are two or three really big attractions. No one can tell how many there will be for you. But the massive magnetic attractions that are connected to one's sense of real purpose on Earth are few rather than many. We want to get in touch with those big magnetic forces and start to dance with them. See where they take us. We are like a couple on the dance floor. The attraction leads and we follow.

When I was in high school, my best friend Homer had an idea for meeting girls. His mother was a dance teacher and she wanted him to take lessons. Dancing didn't interest Homer in the least. But he reasoned that the classes would be filled with girls, and that if I took the classes with him, we'd both meet more young ladies than a handsome high school quarterback at a cheerleader convention.

We decided to take tap dancing lessons because we didn't have to wear leotards and ballet shoes. We were terrible students. We didn't practice. We didn't pay attention and we got into a lot of trouble. But what we did do very well was show off. When it was our turn to demonstrate what we'd learned, we would improvise a comically ridiculous impersonation of what we should have been doing. The girls thought it was hilarious. They would laugh and smile and look us in the eye as we strutted back to our place in line. For about two minutes in every dance class we were the center of attention in a room full of pretty girls. Even Homer's mom couldn't help laughing at our antics.

But Homer loved playing basketball more than anything else. After a couple of months he quit dancing and joined the basketball team at his high school. He was following his attraction, something even bigger than impressing girls. Having already paid for a month of lessons in advance, I continued for the last few weeks on my own. Showing off without Homer wasn't the same so I tried to learn how to tap dance. I stopped noticing the girls. I started listening to the teacher. When the month was over, Homer's mom suggested that I come an hour earlier to take the ballet class that was right before the tap dancing. She said it would help me understand more of the dance terminology.

This was the moment of truth, the potential turning point. Would I follow the attraction or not? In the working class town of Toledo, Ohio, in the 1970s, only girls took dancing lessons. I went downtown and bought a pair of tights, a leotard and the only pair of men's ballet shoes in my city of 300,000 people.

I studied jazz dance, modern dance and ballroom dancing as well as tap and ballet. It was my passion through my teenage years and I became a dance teacher myself in my 20s. I opened my own school and I had a dance partner that I performed with. Her name was Ginger. It was perfect. I even thought of changing my name to Fred.

Even if I had never done anything professionally with dance, it still would have remained one of the big sea grass attractions, the big magnetic forces in my life. Because dancing represents for me the purest non-verbal expression of what I feel inside. I am a dancer. And I found this part of myself and my destiny by following the simple adolescent desire to impress girls.

Timing is very important. If you don't follow the magnetic force of your heart's desire, it might mean that you simply are not be ready. I was in Morocco at the age of 17 with another friend from high school, Jeff Kander. We ended up in the exotic medieval city of Fez, the place that gives its name to the red hat with a tassel worn by Shriners and shady characters in Humphrey Bogart movies. Jeff was a real risk taker and up for almost anything. Those crazy few weeks with Kander whetted my appetite for the mysterious allure of Islamic culture. We were only seven hours from the edge of the Sahara Desert. But we didn't go. I was not ready to embark on my odyssey across the largest and emptiest place on Earth.

When deciding whether or not to follow your heart, consider whether it is the right time to do that. Maybe you can't follow it immediately – you need to prepare or make some changes. But don't let go of it. Dream of it. Carry with you the feeling, the want, the image of the attraction and the desire to follow when the time is right to do so.

If you are unsure about following your compass, you can dip your toe in the water and see what happens. There is an old saying, "Take one step toward the gods and the gods take ten steps toward you."

Here the word "gods" means your destiny. If you follow an attraction for a little bit, if you take some small action that clearly shows you are willing to head in a certain direction, you may be surprised by what happens. The "gods" might take ten steps toward you and suddenly you find that things go well, you start meeting people who support you in following the attraction and you feel encouraged that you have made the right choice.

Or, the opposite can happen, but that doesn't automatically mean it was a bad idea. You can take one small step in the direction of a new magnetic force and immediately enter a time of challenge. But somehow, the difficulties seem right, like you have fallen into the right kind of trouble. And even though it's not easy, you still have the sense that engaging with that challenge keeps you heading in the right direction.

Following our hearts can get us into plenty of trouble but never following them is the worst kind of dilemma. It doesn't always have to be a dramatic life change when you start following an attraction. Sometimes a small but concrete step in the new direction is all it takes for the "gods" to take ten steps toward you, and then the real journey begins.

3

FIND YOUR GIFT

The hawksbill is the most beautiful of all sea turtles. It also has the rare ability to eat and digest sponges. We think of sponges as soft squishy plants but they are actually a primitive animal with sharp glass-like needles forming an external skeleton. Sponges hold strong chemicals that are toxic to most predators. They are so dangerous that smaller fish hide inside and around them for protection from enemies. Yet the hawksbill can grow to a weight of 150 pounds on a steady diet of something other sea creatures assiduously avoid.

With the sharp beak that gives it its name, the hawksbill can tear off bits of sponge without being injured. In addition to providing a food source for which there are few competitors, eating sponges has another advantage – hawksbill meat is poisonous due to the toxic chemicals from the sponges in its diet. Neither humans nor sea predators are interested in a meal of hawksbill turtle.

All modern sea turtles have evolved unique abilities that have helped them survive for the last 200 million years. They are strong and gifted swimmers. Some species can reach speeds of more than 20 miles per hour. They are some of the deepest diving vertebrates on Earth, rivaling the great whales with the depths of their dives. And their navigational abilities are unequalled in the animal world.

Hawksbill sea turtle (Eretmochelys imbricata)

Sea turtles are not at ease on land. They can no longer move with swiftness and agility. It is hard work and they are vulnerable. For thousands of years human turtle hunters have waited for them on the beaches of tropical nesting sites. It is no wonder that hatchlings run as quickly as they can to the safety of the sea. They are sea creatures who by a quirk of nature must come ashore to bury their eggs.

Male sea turtles will never touch land except for those few feet of tropical sand they quickly cross upon hatching. Females will spend 99.99% of their lives in the sea. If water is where they excel and land is where they struggle, we can say that sea turtles spend almost every minute of every day doing what they are natural geniuses at doing – swimming, diving, navigating and in the case of the hawksbill, eating sponges. Look at how perfectly sea turtles are suited for their lives at sea. They have all their necessary talents from the moment they are hatched.

છ

YOU TOO WERE BORN with a unique set of talents that are perfectly suited for the life you were meant to live. Those innate abilities are linked to your destiny, to help you live a specific life and succeed by making the best use of those inherent gifts.

Of course, it always helps to work hard. But working hard at improving, refining, focusing your unique set of natural talents will take you much farther then putting all of your energy into something you don't like or don't have any natural ability for.

I once met a woman named Azura who wanted to become a doctor. Her father was a doctor and all throughout high school and university she thought that she too would become a doctor.

She took the medical school entrance examination. Her results were nothing special, just good enough to be accepted. But she scored in the 99th percentile on the English language portion of the test. She was in the top 1% of all North Americans.

When she received the test results, she realized that she had a remarkable gift for the English language. So she changed the direction of her education to follow the compass of her natural talent. Rather than working very, very hard to become an average medical doctor, she has focused on her talent and become an excellent writer and actress.

You cannot excel at something simply because you work hard. Excellence requires talent. Without talent you can be merely good enough, average at best. Your greatest success will always come from applying your natural and unique abilities in the situations where they have the most impact.

Consider the example of Michael Jordan. He is widely acclaimed as the greatest basketball player of all time. He won five MVP awards, ten scoring titles, three steals titles, and six NBA Finals MVP awards. He holds the NBA records for highest career regular season scoring average and highest career playoff scoring average. He led the Chicago Bulls to victory in six NBA Championships. ESPN voted

Michael Jordan "the greatest North American athlete of the 20th century."

In the prime of his career Michael Jordan retired from basketball. His team had already won three of those NBA championships. His father, who had recently died, had always wanted him to be a professional baseball player. Jordan set out to honor his father's wishes and achieve that goal. More than anything else, at this particular point in his life, he wanted to play major league baseball.

Jordan brought to his baseball career the same competitiveness and desire to be the best that had helped him succeed in basketball. Blessed with some of the greatest natural athletic talent we have ever seen and a warrior's mindset for victory at any cost, Michael Jordan could do no better than bat .202 while striking out 104 times in his only season with a minor league team in Alabama. Compared to the heights he had reached throwing a ball through a netted hoop, Michael Jordan was a complete and utter failure on the baseball diamond.

His rare athletic talent was not universally applicable. In fact, his abilities were very specific. He was meant to play basketball. No matter how hard he tried he would never succeed as a baseball player. He returned to the sport of his destiny with more energy and determination after a difficult year on dusty ball diamonds in the southern United States. Jordan promptly led the Chicago Bulls to three more consecutive NBA championships.

SPEND MORE TIME IN THE WATER AND LESS ON LAND

Think of how difficult it must be for the sea turtle when it drags its massive body onto the beach. No longer buoyant, it feels the full effects of gravity. What a tremendous effort it must exert to drag its massive bulk along the beach, scraping and pushing a small hill of sand in front of it. But we can be just like turtles on land. We try to succeed by working very hard in situations that do not take advantage of our natural talent and abilities.

What percentage of your day is like a sea turtle in the sea? How much of your time feels like you are gliding through the ocean with ease, diving 3,000 feet on a single breath and effortlessly returning to the surface? What amount of your precious allotment of time do you spend doing what you are naturally gifted at doing?

On the other hand, how much of your day feels like you are dragging the almost impossible weight of your massive shell across wet sand? Many of the people I meet spend more of their time doing more of the things that feel like the turtle on the beach, not the turtle in the sea. That approach takes them away from, not closer to, their destiny.

What are you naturally good at doing? What are the situations where you can take the most advantage of your natural talents? How can you spend more time using your unique, inherent abilities and less time struggling with things you have no talent for? If you can answer these questions, you will have a powerful compass heading that can lead you directly to your destined life.

FIND AND DESCRIBE THE BEAUTY OF YOUR SHELL

Have you ever seen beautiful jewelry made from tortoise shell? Perhaps it was a pair of your grandmother's earrings or a necklace that she wore. Maybe you've come across an exquisite antique fan, comb or jewelry box crafted from this precious natural material. If you have seen any of these breathtaking works of art, one thing is certain: A hawksbill turtle was the source of the raw material. Virtually all jewelry and fine crafted ornamental objects made of tortoise shell come from our little sponge-eating friend.

Since the ancient Egyptians, the hawksbill has been prized for only one reason – the staggering beauty of its shell. After it was hunted nearly to extinction in the 20th century, a treaty was enacted in 1977 banning the sale of tortoise shell. It had little effect until Japan finally signed the agreement in 1992, which has nearly halted the trade in hawksbill shells. With a little more luck and more countries signing and enforcing the treaty, this species of living art will survive for many centuries to come.

&

EACH OF US possesses a gift as rare and beautiful as the shell of the hawksbill sea turtle. Our gift shimmers in the light and dazzles the eye when we display this unique talent or ability. Unfortunately, for many of us, we simply do not know what this gift is. We can't see it. Just like the turtle is unable to bend its neck around far enough to see how impressive its shell is, we struggle to recognize what our own beauty might be.

Ironically, one of the best ways to identify your own unique abilities is by noticing the gift that others have. When you receive good service at a restaurant or see someone excelling in sports or art, when a colleague at work or a student shows natural talent in a particular area, try and identify what their gift is. Be as specific as possible when you describe what it is that they are very good at. This sharpens your own observational powers. It puts the task of identifying talent on your radar. Ultimately, you can turn that radar on yourself and tune into your own special gifts.

Having another person such as a teacher, boss, friend or colleague point out in specific terms what natural talents you possess is probably the single most powerful experience for clarifying what unique abilities you have. Unfortunately, it is a far too rare occurrence. I often conduct a survey when I'm speaking to a large audience, asking if anyone has ever had their gift specifically recognized and named by someone else. On average, about 5% of the audience acknowledge experiencing this powerful moment of destiny.

But it never hurts to ask. I once sent an email to ten people – friends, teachers, colleagues and mentors – asking them what they noticed as my unique, inherent talents and abilities. I asked them to be as specific as possible in describing any gift they thought I had. I did not request a critical analysis of my faults and how I could improve. I wanted to simply know what my genius might be as perceived by people who knew me in a variety of different ways. Some responders asked to reply anonymously. So I had a mutual friend collect the information and forward it to me without names attached. I highly recommend this exercise as a powerful first step to understanding your compass heading as based on your natural talents.

You can't wait your whole life for someone to tell you what your destiny is. Ultimately, it becomes your own responsibility to discover your gifts and follow them as your compass. Begin by observing where, when and how you succeed. Success in any form can be a clue to your destiny and a compass direction that you should follow.

Try to remember examples of being successful in the past. Perhaps you received a high score on a test or project at school. Maybe you performed in a play and were the star of the production or you won a sports competition. Were you given new responsibilities at work and suddenly realized you had a natural ability to succeed in a different area? Sometimes we demonstrate talent as a child but it is ignored or misunderstood by our parents and teachers. Make a note of any success or hint of ability. Develop a long list with as many examples as possible.

Start noticing in the present whenever you do something really well. If you cook a fabulous meal for friends or family, put that success on your list. If you listen to a colleague who has a problem and help him or her figure out what to do, put that on your list. If you sell more insurance or more cell phones than everyone else on your team, then put that success on your list. The bigger and more diverse your list of successes, the better your chance of isolating and naming the inherent talents you possess.

Focus on giving a name to your gifts – the more specific the better. Perhaps you analyzed a success and decided that you are "creative." But try to accurately describe just how you are "creative." Maybe you demonstrated the ability to "think creatively while under pressure." That is a more specific description of your talent and will ultimately be more effective when it comes to following your compass.

Don't confuse the situation with your innate ability. Let's say that you scored very high in a certain school subject, like history. But you don't like history. It's boring. What you did do is you really worked hard to study for tests. You memorized an impressive amount of dates and names. You didn't enjoy it but you did not give up and achieved some very high marks. In that situation, we can name your talents as "persistent" or "determined" or "good at memorization." Those are very positive talents that can help you succeed in many areas. But in this situation your gift has little to do with history.

Another good idea for discovering your gifts is to try new things. Follow the magnetic pull of new activities that you are attracted to. You can even try new things for the sake of trying them, even if you don't feel any particular attraction. Sometimes the attraction or the talent can't be noticed until you actually do the new thing. It is worthwhile doing one completely new activity every month. Most of us get stuck in the maps of our lives and we have the same schedules and tasks day after day. Expose yourself to many different challenges so that you will have a chance to see what your unique abilities are.

As you develop a long list of talents and natural abilities, you'll notice that your gift is stronger in some areas than others. Focus on developing and exploring your talent where it is strongest. Another important thing to do with the list is to look for themes, patterns and similarities among the different activities and areas where you have some natural ability. When you identify a consistent and recurring theme in your unique abilities, that is certainly a compass heading to explore.

Don't restrict your search to supposedly practical talents you can use on a job. Many of our gifts are too undeveloped to appear at work or even school. Look far outside of job and education to see what your natural talent is. The next section will show you how to find the right place for your genius once you know what it is.

GIVE YOUR GIFT WHERE IT HAS THE GREATEST IMPACT

Hawksbill sea turtles spend a lot of time around coral reefs because sponges often share the same habitat. Until recently, little was known about the relationship between hawksbills, reefs and sponges. Research is now showing that sponges can compete with coral and, left unchecked, can completely destroy a reef.

Because of their unique diet, hawksbills maintain the balance of delicate coral reef ecosystems. We know that reefs have declined significantly in the last 50 years in parallel with the drop in hawksbill numbers. Not only is this turtle a living work of art but it helps protect the beauty of our ocean's coral reefs. It has found the environment that not only supports it but is a place where the turtle's unique talent does the most good.

Once discovered, we will see that our gifts can be raw or undeveloped and we need to train, hone and perfect them. But the biggest challenge can be finding the right place, opportunity or situation to deliver your gift to the world. When *Shifting Sands* was released, the foreign rights were sold to publishers in countries such as Russia, Turkey, Greece and South Korea. It quickly became clear that South Koreans were buying more copies of my book than all the other countries combined. Sales there are still quite brisk and over 100,000 copies are in print. I realized I was having a greater impact in one place over the others. So I decided to focus on that place. I wrote a book just for South Koreans and now travel there regularly for speaking tours. I've even learned to speak some of their language to further increase my impact when I'm there.

Impact is not merely a matter of quantity. I have a friend who is a magnificent teacher. She could be addressing large university audiences with hundreds of students. But she chooses to work in a maximum security prison instructing women who will be behind bars for many years, some for the rest of their lives. She has a greater impact in terms of the quality of the change that she facilitates in that small group of prisoners than she would experience in the less personal realm of teaching large numbers of more advantaged individuals. And she loves what she does. It's good for her to work in the prison.

Think back to what happens for the hawksbill in the coral reef. It benefits as much as the reef does when it eats the sponges. Your gift should "feed" you when you give it in situations that have impact. Delivering your talents to the world should not only benefit others but it should benefit you from the experience of giving. The energy that you are putting out loops back to you as well.

BEWARE OF PARENTS NAMING GIFTS

What if your daughter is destined to become the greatest mountain climber of all time? Would you be able to encourage her to pursue such a dangerous destiny? One of the most important jobs of a parent is to keep their child safe. If the child is demonstrating a gift for something potentially dangerous, many parents will naturally guide their offspring toward something safer.

Another problem is the un-lived life of the parent. Unfulfilled dreams of parents and their own gifts that were not recognized or developed can be seen in their child even if they don't exist there. When I was born, I was a very big baby, weighing nearly 10 pounds. To my father, a gifted athlete who was not able to pursue a professional career, I was going to be the next superstar American football player. I was only one day old and my dad had named my gift and my destiny. Little did he realize I'd start taking dance lessons in high school!

Teachers, coaches, mentors, uncles, aunts, bosses, grandparents, almost anyone in a position of respect who is not the parent, are often in a good position to notice and name a gift. Perhaps it is because this person, not being the parent, can see more clearly what talent is truly present in the child rather than what the parent hopes or wants to be there.

Parents can help their children the most by seeking to understand what their own gifts are and following those natural talents as their own compass. Let your children see that you have your own unique abilities and that it matters to you to develop those abilities and use them wherever you can to make a difference in the world.

Parents can talk to their kids about the things the children like to do and feel that they can do well. Whenever possible, support them and encourage them to get better at things that they like. But try not to force them to pursue a path in life that simply allows you to feel better about yourself. One of the great challenges of being a parent is to ultimately release your kids to their own destiny while still loving them as they discover their gifts and follow their compass.

4
___

MAKE MORE MISTAKES

The loggerhead is a big bruiser of a sea turtle. Similar in size to the green turtle, it can weigh up to 450 pounds. It gets its name from the large head and massive jaws that it uses to crush the shells of crabs, clams, conches and other well protected food sources.

The loggerhead is the best known and most studied of all the sea turtle species. One of the things scientists have learned is to keep their distance when a female loggerhead is laying her eggs. Unlike other species, a loggerhead will snap with her massive jaws at a researcher taking measurements or trying to count her eggs as they are deposited. This nasty demeanor has probably saved many loggerhead offspring from the brazen poachers that will literally scoop the eggs from the nests of greens or leatherbacks as they are being laid.

Like other turtle species, the loggerhead possesses its own unique talents for survival. But there is one curious trait that appears to be completely disadvantageous. Their shells are home to over 100 different species of hitch-hiking sea animals like barnacles and crabs. In addition to that unwelcome weight, at least 37 different types of algae can take up residence on a loggerhead carapace. These freeloaders create drag and make swimming more difficult for the turtle. Scientists have been unable to explain what benefit the loggerheads might gain from functioning as a floating reef. It appears to be an evolutionary mistake.

As individuals, turtles make plenty of mistakes as well. When I watched the loggerheads hatch on the beach in Florida, the first thing that they did was make a mistake. Instead of crawling toward the safety of the water, they went in the wrong direction toward the highway along the beach. This was a potentially fatal error.

Loggerhead sea turtle (Caretta caretta)

Leatherback sea turtles swallow plastic bags after misjudging them for the jellyfish that comprise most of their diet. Navigational errors can put turtles in strong ocean currents that carry them thousands of miles away from feeding grounds and nesting sites. Sea turtles native to the warm waters of the Caribbean are sometimes found off the coast of Great Britain. One can only imagine the many mistakes a sea turtle makes while trying to follow its compass over the course of a lifetime.

Yet each year at nesting sites all over the world sea turtles return, having survived not only their own wrongdoing but the great threat of human predation. Sea turtles and their ancestors have been making mistakes and surviving them for a long time. They were here before the dinosaurs and they are still here in spite of the dangers they face and the mistakes they make.

ε.

MISTAKES ARE essential to the journey of destiny. We can follow the wrong direction. We can misinterpret our compass signals. We can leave a nest too soon or too late. We can misunderstand our gift or use it in the wrong situation. There are lots of mistakes to make. Reading this book will not reduce the amount of faux pas you'll commit. Ideally, you will make more mistakes, not fewer.

When I was a child, my parents had a Polish friend who played the accordion. Every time Mr. Wanucha strapped on his accordion the party would come to life. The polka music would cast its spell and everyone would begin dancing. I was fascinated with the strange but beautiful instrument he played. I knew that some day I too would play the accordion.

At the age of 53 I finally started taking lessons. It was the first time since I was a teenager that I was pursuing any formal music training. It was not easy. I couldn't practice often due to my constant travel. I would get nervous playing in front of my teacher. The fear of making mistakes caused me to make even more mistakes.

I decided I would play a song at one of my speaking engagements, a conference for internal auditors. I thought that the pressure to perform in front of 400 accountants would inspire me to practice harder. And since I'm always telling people to take a risk, to do the thing they're afraid to do, I was now walking the talk. I was clearly terrified about my first public accordion performance.

I managed to make one great, big, fat mistake in the middle of the song. Nobody laughed but I could see everyone wince when I played a series of wrong notes. I doubt I will ever play an accordion during a speech again. But I learned something very important that day – accordion mistakes are not fatal.

AVOID ONLY THE DEADLY MISTAKES

There are two very important differences between humans and sea turtles when it comes to mistakes. First of all, very few, if any, of the mistakes we make are potentially deadly. Yet we fear making them as if every possible error could cost us our life. Secondly, unlike a sea turtle, we know that mistakes exist and can be avoided. So we spend a lot of time and effort trying to avoid wrongdoing. But when it comes to following our compass, we need to be a lot more like sea turtles and take the chance that something will go wrong.

Most mistakes made by following your compass are not dangerous at all. We are simply afraid of making mistakes. We are afraid of being less than perfect. But perfection would be the experience of living your destiny. A perfect life, or something close to perfection, would include growing into your greatest potential, using your gifts where they have the most impact, following your own unique compass rather than a map drawn by someone else. Paradoxically, this type of perfection is only realized through making mistakes.

Start making more mistakes. Give yourself permission to get it wrong when it comes to your compass. Learning to understand the signals from your heart and guide your life from the depth of your core is not easy. No one has the map. You learn by doing it and that means there will be mistakes.

MAKE MISTAKES EARLY

Look how quickly things go wrong for turtle hatchlings as they emerge from the sand and try to find the sea. In fact, the mother turtle can mess things up right from the start. If she lays her eggs below the high tide line, the sand will be too cool to incubate them. If she buries her eggs in a shallow nest, predators will find them. Or, she can bury the eggs too deep, making it difficult for the hatchlings to dig their way out. Mistakes are part of sea turtle life from the very beginning.

Since mistakes are often made at the beginning of doing something new, this fear can freeze us and stop us from moving forward because we understand that within a few steps in the new direction we'll get the chance to mess it up. As important as it is to follow attractions or follow your gift, I can promise you that much of the time the right direction to head is the one that frightens you the most. The fear of being imperfect will keep us trapped in our nests and the journey will never begin. Rather than avoid mistakes we should be expecting to make them right away whenever we set forth on a new journey away from our beach.

I spent 10 years thinking about writing my first book. I was afraid that it would be full of mistakes. I had not written a thing since I left high school decades ago. So I made plans to take courses in creative writing. But I never found the time or the commitment to take the courses and the years passed without any book or even a paragraph being written. Ten years went by because I was afraid that it wouldn't be perfect.

Then one day I attended a seminar by a speaker named Marcia Martin. After the lecture was over I started complaining about not being able to write my book. Marcia said, "Anything worth doing is worth doing poorly." I corrected her by explaining that she had the proverb backwards – "Anything worth doing is worth doing well." Marcia explained that doing something that we were meant to do, even if we did it poorly at first, was much better than never doing it at all because we feared being less than perfect. Thanks to her backwards proverb I began to follow my compass and wrote my first book. It was not perfect but it became an international bestseller. It would never have been written if I hadn't realized that following an attraction would always require making mistakes. Now I try making them a lot sooner.

One of my favorite poets is an American named William Stafford. He was famous for writing a poem every day of his adult life. A younger poet once asked Stafford how he managed to be so productive. The young man explained that it took him weeks to write a single poem, fussing over each and every word until he was finally satisfied with the work. Stafford's advice on writing more was blunt: "Lower your standards."

Over a 50-year career William Stafford composed almost 22,000 poems. Did Stafford publish 22,000 poems? Of course not. But the ones he did publish are a great treasure of modern English poetry and they would not exist if he didn't follow his own advice. Stafford was not afraid to make a mistake.

FIND THE OPPORTUNITY IN THE MISTAKE

Loggerheads spend the first six to ten years of their lives far out at sea. They drift in ocean currents feeding on animals and insects that live in large floating mats of algae. Upon reaching half their adult size the turtles move onshore to shallow water. They begin bottom feeding on the large mollusks that will comprise the bulk of their diet for the rest of their lives. Unfortunately, they are now in the direct path of fishing trawlers, especially shrimp boats, dragging their nets along the sea bottom.

Shrimp trawling has long been considered the leading cause of death for sea turtles. Scientists estimate that until recently, as many as 50,000 loggerheads died each year in American waters alone as part of unintentional catches by shrimp trawlers. Loggerheads are especially vulnerable since they live in the same onshore waters as shrimp. But all species of sea turtle have been decimated by shrimp fishing.

Some countries now require shrimp trawlers to install a Turtle Excluder Device (TED) on the end of their nets. The TED is a trap door, an escape hatch that allows the turtle, or any other large sea creature, to swim away free and unharmed. I have seen underwater videos of this remarkable device showing the turtle swimming deeper and deeper into the quickly narrowing net. Just before it enters the final closed end where all the shrimp are accumulating, the turtle bumps a large metal grate which forces it out an opening on the side of the net. The turtle escapes. The shrimp don't.

It would be a much safer world for turtles if there were no shrimp trawlers. It would be great if we didn't make mistakes on the way to our destiny. But there is a way to come out the other side of a mistake much as a turtle does, in good shape, perhaps even better condition than when we went in.

To find the escape hatch out of a mistake means something positive will happen. Mistakes are a golden opportunity for change, transformation, learning, growth and compass clarity. A little-known benefit of mistakes is that they can give you energy, a boost, better focus and more determination.

My son is a gifted soccer player. One thing Spirit has always done well is pass the ball. He sees the developing play and chooses the right player to pass the ball to at the right time. Sometimes he passes the ball when it would have been better to use his own footwork and foot speed to carry it forward himself. But this is riskier. The defender can take the ball away from him and it would look like a mistake on my son's part to not have passed. I have wondered if sometimes he made the pass to avoid making the mistake.

I encouraged him to hang onto the ball and try to advance it himself. When he would lose the ball to the defender, it made him angry and he would try very hard to recover it from the player who had taken it away. Spirit would try with considerably more effort to get the ball back than he would use to keep the ball from being stolen in the first place. I realized that mistakes have power; they contain energy and present an opportunity to do something positive.

Think about a time when you made a mistake and then discovered a new surge of energy that the mistake released. Most likely the energy went toward fixing the problem you created or making someone feel better because you had let them down. But it's essential to understand that the energy from the mistake can be focused in any direction you choose. Think about a different way that you could have used the energy from the mistake. Try to imagine something else that could have happened in addition to the efforts you made in righting the wrong.

In the last chapter I described Michael Jordan's mistake quitting basketball to become a professional baseball player. I wonder how much energy that mistake released? Could he have returned to basketball and led the Chicago Bulls to three more championships without that mistake? We can never know for sure, but I suspect that his error had a lot to do with his renewed drive for future success.

In the world of sea turtles many mistakes are deadly. That's why a turtle nest contains 100 or more eggs. Hatchlings that survive to adulthood have made many mistakes and learned from them. Those clever enough to make it to the age of reproduction pass their DNA to the next generation. As humans, most of our mistakes are not fatal. But if fear of making mistakes prevents us from following our compass, then a certain type of death has befallen us – the loss of living the life we were meant to live. If we overcome this fear and use the energy of mistakes to accelerate our speed along the true path of our lives, then we too will pass something very powerful to the next generation. We will show them that anyone can fulfill the great promise of their deep and mysterious destiny.

5

DIVE DEEP

Six of the seven sea turtle species belong to the same family, *cheloniidae*. The only member of the *dermochelyidae* family is the leatherback. This fascinating behemoth belongs in a class of its own. It can grow to three, even four times the size of the largest green turtle or loggerhead, with some leatherbacks weighing over 2,000 pounds. It is not only the largest turtle but one of the largest reptiles in the world.

It is the fastest swimmer of all sea turtles and extremely agile for its size. A leatherback can easily outmaneuver a shark if threatened. This majestic mariner migrates farther than any other turtle species and forages for food in the widest range. Its unique fatty tissue allows it to maintain a warm body temperature even in cold waters near the Arctic Ocean. The leatherback is such an unusual and fascinating creature that it was placed in the same category as mythical sea serpents until a French scientist classified it as a turtle in the 16th century.

Sea turtles are magnificent divers. But when it comes to the deepest dives, size makes the difference. The leatherback easily matches the great whales with dives that surpass 3,000 feet on just a single breath of air. It has evolved unique characteristics to survive the depth and duration of its dives. Unlike other sea turtles, the leatherback does not have a hard shell. The thick leathery skin on its back, from which it derives its name, is flexible and more suitable for coping with the increased pressure. It also has collapsible lungs and a slower heart rate for conserving oxygen.

Leatherbacks eat jellyfish, which are concentrated near the surface. For that reason most of their dives are less than 1,000 feet. But about one percent of the time they will probe the darkest ocean waters at depths exceeding half a mile. Using satellite transmitter-derived data scientists have been able to confirm the extraordinary feat of the leatherbacks. But no one has been able to explain the purpose of these deepest dives. We may never know the real reason why this gargantuan sea turtle plumbs such remarkable depths. All we know is that from time to time the turtles are compelled to go deep and there is good reason for you to do the same.

DIVING deep in our lives means that we are getting beneath the surface of everyday motivation, superficial understanding, mundane thoughts and automatic reactions. We are trying to set aside our maps and connect with our mysterious compass signals. When we go deep, we are trying to see, sense or feel what our heart truly wants, what our pain really means and where our destiny is trying to take us.

We all experience times in life when we are forced to dive deep. Something happens to upset the predictability, comfort or security of our lives. The map we've been following stops working. Maybe you will suddenly be struggling with your marriage or your job. The economy could deteriorate or your health could change without warning. Something unexpected sends you plunging to the dark hidden places inside of you in search of answers to your dilemma. As difficult as they may be, these times of challenge and change also present great opportunities for accessing the deep direction and motivations of your destiny.

LEARN TO HOLD YOUR BREATH

All sea turtles can spend several hours under water if they are resting. But the deep dives of leatherbacks require effort and oxygen. Studies have shown that these giants can still spend up to 48 minutes under water from a single breath that carries them to depths more than half a mile beneath the surface. These increasingly rare behemoths, which are sadly nearing extinction in the Pacific, are clearly the masters of the deep.

Leatherback sea turtle (Dermochelys coriacea)

Like a leatherback, I've always been good at holding my breath. I can swim for long distances underwater. I remember one time being at a public swimming pool and playing a game with my kids to see who could hold their breath the longest while floating. I held my breath for so long that a lifeguard jumped in the water to rescue me, thinking that I might be drowning. I have even considered participating in the sport of free diving, where contestants holding heavy weights descend hundreds of feet and return to the surface in a single breath.

Whenever we feel low in life, our instinct is to feel up again as quickly as possible. We're uncomfortable going deep emotionally or psychologically. We don't want to get caught down there and run out of "breath." But difficult times in life, those times when we feel "down," are often the very best times to reflect on the direction of our life and find our compass. We can take the opportunities of feeling unhappy, depressed, sad, lonely, anything that makes you feel "down," as the chance to dive deeper. Use the difficult situation to take you deeper, like the weight that pulls the free diver to record depths. Try to understand what it is that you really want, what you really need, what the deepest heart of you is trying to draw you toward. But most importantly, try to stay down there on purpose. Learn to hold your breath.

Why would anyone want to remain any longer than necessary in a difficult or painful situation? Well, this is not about being passive and accepting that nothing will ever improve. I'm suggesting that it is only within the increased pressure of the great depths of our challenging times that certain kinds of things will ever change. Being down in our depths is the chance to discover the foundational truths of our soulful destiny. It's the place where no maps work. It is in the dark of such depths that our hands often grasp the compass we need or the treasure that we seek in vain on the surface of everyday life.

In tough times we often take deep breaths to calm ourselves. The next time you find yourself doing that, remember to metaphorically hold that breath. Stay down there a little longer. Have a look around. You are in a new world: Use that opportunity to find out more about who you are and where you need to go. Then kick swiftly back the surface.

COMMIT 1% OF YOUR TIME TO DIVING DEEP

Don't wait for the tough times to deepen yourself. While you should take advantage of those periods when they occur, it also makes sense to develop a regular practice that connects you to your core while also preparing you to cope with those unexpected moments when everything gets turned inside-out. I recommend that you spend one percent of your time diving into the depths of your inner world.

Reading a book like this might be your way to go deep. I have friends who use meditation to access the profound center of their existence. For many years, the first thing I would do when I woke up was to write in a journal about how I felt and what I wanted. I did it every day and my intention was to write my deepest thoughts and feelings as a way of finding my true compass heading.

What I'm describing is a daily practice. I'm suggesting that it takes approximately one percent of your time, about 10 or 15 minutes a day. We don't know why the leatherback sea turtle dives extraordinarily deep, but we do know that it does it about one percent of the time. Can you do the same?

One of my best friends, Renée Coleman, has a PhD in psychology but she calls herself a DreamTender. Her clients keep a pen and notepad close to their bed. When they wake up in the middle of the night or first thing in the morning, they record any dreams that they can remember. Renée's clients learn how to follow the images from their own dreams to help understand what the very deepest part of their psyche is trying to tell them. I have also tried this daily depth practice and some of the biggest turning points in my life have been linked to a dream that I dreamt.

Writing free verse poetry allows me to access and express deep feelings and beliefs. Quite often I'm surprised by what words appear on the paper. There is a stark truth and raw emotionality that I am unable to feel or describe other than by writing a poem. I'm not sure that everyone would have this result but this too could become your own daily depth practice.

Reading or even memorizing poetry could be another way to go deep. A powerful poem memorized is like a treasure that you found in the depths and carry inside of you wherever you go. Prayer or some other devotional practice could help you go deep every day. It doesn't matter what it is as long as it works for you and as long as you do it every day for 10 or 15 minutes.

You could have a weekly deep dive instead of daily plunges. One percent of your time would equal an hour or an hour and a half per week. Maybe you could set aside that time to simply reflect on your life or any particular issue you're facing. You could go for a hike up a mountain. At the top you can write in your journal what you thought about. At the bottom you can write what decisions you made or changes you want to attempt.

One percent of a month would be about seven hours. How about an annual, one percent extended dive? That would be three full days. How could you spend that time getting closer to the core purpose that lives inside you?

Most of the practices I've described have been solitary experiences. But you don't need to dive alone. You could attend a self–development seminar led by an author or teacher that you like. You could form a group of friends who are interested in recording and interpreting their dreams and work together once a week with the help of a trained dream therapist.

If you are in a long-term committed relationship, go deeper with that person as a way of strengthening your connection and clarifying the purpose you share as a couple. This kind of practice can be very simple. You can find a book about relationships or a book of love poems and read aloud to each other for 15 minutes before you go to bed. The content of what you read is almost secondary to the commitment to do it together and allow the experience to take both of you deeper into the love and destiny you share.

For several years I went to a weekly class on improvisational acting. This was a great depth practice for me because it was all about reacting to what another actor has said or done. There is no preparation whatsoever. There is no script, only certain rules that govern the "game" that you are playing. Having little or no time to think about what I was going to say would often cause something very unusual and yet very honest to come from a very deep place within me. And, it was a lot of fun!

Your one percent practice for diving deep doesn't have to be a solitary experience that is hard work, overly serious or fraught with angst. But it needs to be regular. It needs to occupy about one percent of your time. It needs to feel like you are getting in touch with something deeper that is not possible in the busy everydayness of our lives. It requires setting aside time for regular periods devoted exclusively to your practice.

It is important to focus on the conversation with your core, with your heart, and less so on the result or finding answers to every question that you have. This type of practice builds the communication network between you and the mysterious, fiery center of your being. The answers you seek, the new compass directions that you hope for, may emerge at other times quite unexpectedly and quite surprisingly. You might be stuck in rush-hour traffic when out of nowhere, suddenly, you realize the answer to something you've been struggling with. That can happen because the channel has been opened, the communication cable has been laid down and your deeper self is beginning to tell you the truth about who you are and where you're headed.

GET BENEATH THE SURFACE

In *Shifting Sands* I wrote about my friend Tallis, who I crossed the Sahara desert with. It is easy in hindsight to see how the Sahara and especially Tallis are part of my destiny. Without him I would never have crossed the desert. Without Tallis I would never have written that first book. I moved to Canada to be with my friend and it has been my home ever since. Clearly, Tallis has been one of the most important figures in my entire life. I wrote about how we met on the boat from Canada to Europe and that we had lived together in Paris before crossing the desert. But what I did not mention in the book was how Tallis and I almost missed our destiny.

When the Russian passenger liner *SS Alexander Pushkin* docked in France, most of the passengers disembarked and scattered across Europe. I had booked passage to Germany and was unaware that almost everyone, including Tallis, planned to leave the boat in France. I'm sure he expected to see me on that gangplank with the rest of the passengers heading for the trains. But when I woke up late that fateful morning, Tallis was gone. I had no idea where he was or how to find him.

Three days later I arrived in Germany. Alone and lonely, I began hitchhiking south. I wanted to get somewhere warm for the winter like Greece or Southern Italy. Someone offered me a ride to Paris. It was late October and Paris was going to be cold. But something inside me said, "What's the harm? If you don't like Paris, you can keep heading south." So I took the ride.

After a couple of weeks of hanging out and visiting museums I was ready to leave the City of Lights. I hopped on the subway with my backpack heading for the Gare de Lyon to take the famous *Le Mistral* train to the Mediterranean. En route the subway stopped at the Latin Quarter, a cafe district that was very popular with students and young travelers in the 1970s. I was suddenly seized by the idea to get off and have a last look around one of my favorite parts of Paris. But I hesitated. Getting off would mean having to pay again to get back on the subway and continue to the train station. Just before the doors closed I literally dove headfirst off the subway car and tumbled onto the crowded platform. As the throng began to move around me toward the escalators I heard someone call my name. I looked up. It was Tallis.

I cannot prove unequivocally that your destiny will always put you in the right place at the right time to meet the right person for your journey. But things like this have happened many times for me and so I wonder if a force, which is not my conscious intellect, seems to know where I'm headed before I know and thereby helps me get there somehow.

Whenever serendipitous situations appear out of nowhere, it's like your inner compass needle is spinning rapidly, going haywire, getting too much signal because you're in a highly magnetic region. An angel of destiny is knocking on your door, trying to get your attention. You need to dive even deeper before the doors to the opportunity are closed. Searching below the surface of life as a daily, weekly or monthly practice improves your chances of receiving the signals that sometimes nudge you toward an intersection in life. The one percent of your time diving deeper is an investment that can pay off in life-changing ways.

6

RETURN HOME

Upon reaching sexual maturity, sea turtles begin making their way to the beach where they were born. Driven by instinct and guided by their compass, these magnificent navigators have traveled tens of thousands of miles since that fateful day when they hatched on a sandy beach and scampered to their destiny in the sea. Now they are heading home.

For some species it can take a very long time to return to their place of birth. Scientists estimate that loggerheads reach maturity between 12 and 30 years of age. It's even longer for green turtles, as much as 25-50 years. Once sea turtles have begun reproducing, they will continue to return to their natal beach every two or three years for the rest of their lives.

The Kemp's ridley is the smallest of the sea turtle species, weighing about 100 pounds. It is found primarily in the Gulf of Mexico and off the eastern coast of the United States. The mating habits of this reptile were a complete mystery for many decades. How Kemp's ridleys procreated and where, or even if, they laid eggs was one of the great zoological puzzles of the 20th century.

Discovered in 1906 by a Florida fisherman and naturalist, Richard Kemp, this species had never been seen nesting. It was commonly assumed that the Kemp's was a hybrid species, a "mule" of the turtle world, conceived and born at sea from the illicit pairing of a green and a loggerhead.

The Kemp's cantankerous personality makes it the bane of any fisherman forced to reckon with the spitting, biting, hissing and violent thrashing of this small but fierce turtle. Unlike greens, Kemp's ridleys don't travel well in captivity. They are usually dead within a couple of hours of capture. Fishermen call them the heartbreak turtle because they die on their backs from what appears to be a heart attack brought on by their struggle to escape.

Kemp's ridley sea turtle (Lepidochelys kempii)

Inspired by Archie Carr's quest to locate the Kemp's ridley nesting site, another scientist, Henry Hildebrand, began searching as well. In 1960 Hildebrand was told of a film made by an amateur naturalist named Andrés Herrera. Shot in 1947, the footage showed a small stretch of isolated Mexican beach swarming with the nesting females. It was estimated that as many as 42,000 turtles had returned to that beach on a single day. Nearly every Kemp's Ridley on Earth was born on, and returning to, the same minuscule stretch of the Mexican coastline. This astonishing video, which can be found on YouTube, was the clue that pointed Dr. Hildebrand in the right direction.

The mystery had been solved but a new dilemma surfaced. By 1978 the number of nesting females had dropped to only 200. The once thriving and formerly mysterious Kemp's ridley teetered on the edge of extinction. Coming home had all but ceased. The heartbreak turtle was breaking the hearts of turtle lovers around the world.

ॐ

It's sad to think of a world where sea turtles might no longer be. The saga of their migrations to come home to the place where they were born is one of the great epic stories in the animal kingdom. Their annual return to natal beaches can inspire our returns. Like sea turtles, we too must complete our own life journeys by following our compass out into the world and then back to the place that we call home – our inner home.

To most indigenous peoples, home has been their natural environment. Whether it is a quiet flowing river, sunbaked savannah, sacred mountains, towering dunes or steamy rain forest, "home" is the outdoors. But our busy, urban, goal-oriented modern life has made it difficult to claim a natural environment in this way.

The family or ancestral domicile, the village, the building where we were born, is often what we call home. The condo, the apartment, the house, the school residence, wherever it is you sleep at night might also be home to you. Whether it's a room or a building that you come back to at the end of a long day, or the town where you were raised that you now visit once a year, most of us can quickly identify a place or two that means "home" to us.

This chapter is about a different kind of home. This "home" is not so much a physical location on Earth but a sense of arrival or return inside of us. It is the experience of an inner homecoming to the place where we are "born" spiritually or psychologically and where we claim the fruits of our journey. It is a time of returning to our true selves and an experience of living our destiny.

If a sea turtle could think and feel like a human, its first thought upon leaving the nest would be that it was homeless. Adrift in a great dark sea, separated from its siblings and having fled the sandy womb, how could it feel anything else? But humans can certainly feel homeless under far less traumatic circumstances and this is a good place to start so that we can find our way back.

Several years ago my father suffered a serious stroke. I immediately returned to my hometown of Toledo. I stayed for a few days visiting him every day at the hospital. When he stabilized, I told him that I would be back soon. I think he understood me. It was hard to tell because the stroke had affected his ability to speak. I told him I was going to give a speech at a conference in Puerto Rico, a place he loved and had visited many times on business trips. He nodded, and then I left on my speaking tour.

Three days later I was back in Toledo. My dad had taken a turn for the worse. I was driving to the hospital for a meeting with some of my sisters and his doctor. My cell phone rang. It was my eldest sister, Mary, and she asked me where I was. I told her that I was just pulling into the hospital parking lot and she said, "Hurry!"

I parked in the first empty space and jumped out of the car. I started checking my pockets to make sure that I had my wallet and my cell phone and my phone charger. I had a bottle of water in the car and I went to reach for that. Of course I knew that my father was dying but for some reason I felt a strange compulsion to make sure I had everything that I could possibly need. Suddenly, a voice inside my head, a voice I had never heard before, yelled "RUN!!!!"

I ran cross the parking lot, through the parking garage, down the long hallway to the hospital and through a labyrinth of lobbies and doctors' offices toward the elevators. All the while listening to the public address system paging and urging the family members of the patient in room 505 to return immediately. When the elevator doors opened, a nurse was standing in the hallway outside my father's room. She was waving her arms in a circular motion like the third-base coach in a baseball game encouraging the base runner to head for home with the utmost of speed.

The small, private room was dimly lit but I could see four of my sisters around his bed. My Aunt Ellen, Dad's older sister, was there too, a little bit off to the side. Mary was still on the phone trying to reach our brother Dan at work. I squeezed in next to one of my sisters at the bedside and watched our dad as he took the last few breaths of his life.

My father taught me many things – how to catch and throw a baseball, how to drive a car, how to get on an airplane and fly far away to earn a living, how to be a dad, how to be a husband. I have always been afraid of death and dying. But much less so now. My father had just taught me how to die. At the very least, how not to be afraid of dying.

I almost missed his last few moments on Earth by standing in the parking lot checking my pockets. It was puzzling at the time but now I understand my behavior. My mother had died a little more than a year before my dad. The hometown that I returned to every year would never feel the same. Their house had always represented home. Even when they moved to a smaller place, somewhere that I had never lived, it still felt like home. That deep comfort of knowing your parents are still alive even if they live far away was gone. What I was doing in that parking lot was my own bizarre way of making sure I had everything I needed for the journey that was about to begin in room 505 – the journey to find my way home.

FEEL HOMELESS

You don't have to suffer the loss of your parents and their home to feel homeless. The family home is never the inner home. This truth only became clear to me when I lost my mom and dad. Feeling homeless, with respect to our inner journey, is a natural state of modern human existence. If you notice how easy it is to feel homeless and how often it happens, it can inspire your return to the inner abode where you belong while also hastening that journey.

Feeling homeless shows up in many different ways. We can feel lost or lonely. We can feel like we have no friends or no future. We can feel like we're in the wrong place or that we don't belong anywhere. We can feel like no one understands us. Many of our uncomfortable feelings can be traced to what I'm calling inner, spiritual or psychological homelessness. Without it, very few of us would go on the journey in search of our true self and true direction in life. Destiny would not be experienced if not for this yearning to find our inner home.

Deep in the depths of my sorrow I could see things better than when I was up on the surface. Something about losing my dad helped me think and feel more clearly about what really mattered in my life. Two weeks after my father's funeral I ended what had been a difficult relationship and called off the engagement. I couldn't marry another person until I found my way back to myself.

It was November and for the next two months the darkness of the season in the Pacific Northwest mirrored the feelings inside me. I felt cut off from joy and meaning in my life. I had sunk to a great depth and didn't know what to do. I wasn't choosing to stay there. I wasn't holding my breath. I simply couldn't do anything but feel completely alone and utterly homeless.

A few days before Christmas I received an e-mail from Korea. It was from a young man who worked for the Korean Broadcasting System as a documentary film producer. Young Joong Jo had read my first book. He wanted me to take him to the Sahara Desert so he could have an adventure like I had had at his age and he wanted to make a film about it. I was completely stunned by such a request and didn't know what to do. Finally I replied and explained that I had lost both of my parents and was in no position to become a tour guide to a place I hadn't been in over 30 years.

A week later I received another e-mail. Young Joong told me that he wanted to learn about life. He believed that could happen for him in the Sahara Desert like it had happened for me. He was newly married and his wife was pregnant. He didn't know if he was up to the task of being a good husband and a good father. Young Joong said that he needed an older person with the requisite life experience to guide him through his learning adventure. He told me that he would like me to be his guru and that he wanted to become my disciple. Then he asked me again – would I take him to the Sahara?

I tried to get beneath the surface of this situation. This young man and his request had come out of nowhere. But it seemed too coincidental to ignore – he had my attention. More importantly he had touched my heart. I had never been asked so directly to help a young adult find their way. I felt needed and valued. I began to surface from my depths. I realized I needed him too and the trip he was proposing was something long overdue. I decided to go back to the Sahara with Young Joong Jo.

We were on two completely different journeys. He was leaving the nest, heading out to sea, throwing himself into an environment as foreign as possible from what he knew in Korea. I on the other hand was on a pilgrimage. I was returning to the place where I had been psychologically, even spiritually born to my destiny 33 years ago. I was excited to be going back and afraid of what might happen, or that nothing would happen.

I met Young Joong and his cameraman in Paris and we flew to Tamanrasset, an Algerian oasis in the middle of the Sahara Desert. Our plane landed at 2:00 in the morning. We cleared Customs and met our Tuareg guides. Minutes later, as the Koreans were filming the loading of the four-wheel-drive vehicles, they were surrounded by police and soldiers pointing guns at them. The airport was also a military facility and filming was strictly prohibited.

They were taken into the airport for interrogation. I felt a deep sense of foreboding as I remembered my own troubles with Algerian authorities more than three decades ago. An hour passed and I wondered if we would be on the next plane back to Paris. After the second hour I was convinced that my return to the Sahara would go no further than a parking lot. Eventually the sky began to brighten and I was grateful that I would see at least one last Saharan sunrise. Then the sliding doors of the airport opened. One wearied filmmaker and his harried cameraman emerged onto the sidewalk. They had managed to convince the Algerians to release them along with their film gear.

A couple of days later we camped amidst towering dunes that rose a thousand feet above us. It was the most beautiful place on Earth that I had ever seen. As the sun was setting I climbed the ridge of a smaller dune. I looked out over this endless sea of undulating sand mountains and watched as their color changed from yellow to orange to pink and finally a warm glowing brown as the sun finally set.

As we sat around the campfire with the Tuaregs, Young Joong invited me to climb to the peak of the tallest dune to watch the sun rise the next morning. After a few hours of sleep we got up, turned on our headlamps, left camp in darkness and walked across a flat sandy plain to the base of the dune and began to ascend.

Walking in sand is harder than following a path up a mountain but I was surprised by how much my Korean disciple struggled during the ascent. His breathing was labored and he needed to stop often and rest. Young Joong was half my age and it looked like he was close to having a heart attack. I grabbed one of his arms and our head guide, Moulay, grabbed the other. Virginie, the trip organizer and translator, marched behind us with a steady stream of firm and encouraging words. Together we reached the summit just in time for the spectacular sunrise. Young Joong posed for his cameraman as if he'd summited Mt. Everest.

That night, awaiting dinner, everyone was sitting chatting around the fire as had become our routine. Brahim, our cook, had a large bowl and was adding water and flour and mixing it with his right hand. I asked him, "What are you making?" He said, "Tagela, Tuareg bread." "How are you going to bake bread in the middle of the desert?" He said "just like this" and grabbed a branch, brushed away the hot glowing embers, hollowed out a hole in the hot sand and poured the dough into the hole. He covered it with sand and then put the hot coals on top of everything. Without thinking I shouted excitedly, "I've eaten tagela before!"

Suddenly I had all the nomads' attention. They wanted to know how and when I had eaten tagela. And then, beneath a breathtaking canopy of desert stars, in a circle around the fire, I told them the story of the night I'd spent with Tuaregs 33 years ago. It's the same story that I'd been telling for over 20 years as a motivational speaker. I had probably told that story a thousand times in front of hundreds of thousands of people. And now I had brought the story back to them. Or, more likely, the story had brought me back to the desert.

As I was telling the story I felt like those five nomads had been waiting for 33 years, keeping a place by the fire, waiting for me to return. I felt like I had come back to the part of myself that always wanted to be Lawrence of Arabia, the part that I had left behind so many years ago when life got busy and telling stories about the desert became a way to make a living. I felt like I was exactly where I belonged, in the middle of nowhere waiting for bread to bake in the sand. I felt like I actually had something to offer the world and my one and only disciple in the entire world sat next to me as proof of that achievement. I felt like a great turtle who after 33 years at sea had reached maturity and heaved its heavy body back onto land. I had finally come home.

MAKE SURE YOUR ARRIVAL IS NOTICED

The Kemp's ridley turtle and its cousin the olive ridley are the only two species known to nest en masse in the impressive display called "arribada," Spanish for "arrival." It's hard not to notice an arribada. Not only because of the staggering number of turtles nesting at once, but because unlike the other five species, who lay their precious eggs under the cover of darkness, these tiniest of the sea turtles come ashore in broad daylight.

We will likely never see the Kemp's arribada return to its former glory. Having slipped so close to extinction, the arrival of even a single Kemp's now draws great attention as scientists and volunteers patrolling the nesting sites quickly harvest the eggs and transfer them to the safety of fenced corrals for incubation and release. Thankfully, the olives still manage to amaze us with their unimaginable numbers storming the beach at once.

{·

SCIENTISTS HAVE BEEN unable to explain the purpose of the arribada and the daylight nesting. We may never know why Ridleys draw such attention to their arrival. But it is essential to our own journeys of life that the act, the experience, or simply the feeling of arrival be noticed.

The inner homecoming is a moment of finding or remembering, connecting or reconnecting with, claiming or reclaiming an essential part of yourself, a truth about who you are. When you arrive home, wherever you are, it is precisely where you belong, and you are doing what you should be doing. Our own personal arribadas must be noticed because they are literally the experience of living our destiny. When you feel like you've arrived, then your destiny is alive.

In the first chapter I wrote that your inner compass sits in the middle of two mysteries. We don't know exactly what the deep and inner force at the core of our being wants of us and we don't know exactly where we will end up by following this force. But the moment of arrival – a mystery until it is upon us – is the very place that we have been pointed toward by our core and compass.

You do not have to go to the Sahara Desert or wait 33 years for your homecoming. The sense of feeling at home, like you have come back to some essential part of yourself, or truth about who you are, can be experienced more often and more easily. Following any of the concepts in this book can bring you instantly to this point of arrival. Just by leaving a nest you can feel the sense of arribada, like you've arrived immediately just by leaving. Following an attraction, doing something you love to do or using your unique talent can feel like you've come home to your destiny.

I once asked my stepdaughter Siobhan where she felt most at home. Without hesitation she replied, "A barn." She explained that for the last ten years her greatest passion had been riding horses. The simple act of opening a barn door to a stable full of horses immediately brought her to the sensation of coming back to a significant part of who she really is and what she is meant to do.

Even getting into trouble, if it's the right kind of trouble, feels like home. When I am writing a book and my deadline looms, I go through great stress trying to complete my project on time. As the deadline gets closer I work harder and stop socializing. My friends worry about me. But I'm at home, literally, writing in my bed, at the kitchen table or upstairs in the spare room I've turned into an office. But more importantly I'm at home with the trouble I'm in. I've gone out into the world eager to write a book, found a publisher and squeezed myself into a deadline. Anything that makes us feel like we've arrived is something to keep doing.

It may take some practice to recognize when you have made it back to the home inside yourself. You need to notice your own arrival. You need to be able to say, "Ah, this is it. I feel like I've come home." We want to notice what this feels like, remember how we got here and come back as often as we can.

Sometimes we are lucky enough to have another person – a teacher, a friend, a mentor, a colleague, even a parent or relative –

notice when we have come home to ourselves. It would be a very wise and intuitive person who could see this inner arrival in someone else. It would certainly be a person who had experienced the inner homecoming themselves. But even if someone helps you see that you've found your way back to your core, there is still something important to do when your arrival has been noticed.

LET YOUR DESTINY HATCH

There are now about 2,000 Kemp's ridley females nesting annually in the Gulf of Mexico. These are not the arribadas of old, but are much improved since their near extinction in the 1970s. As soon as shrimp trawlers began using Turtle Exclusion Devices and the beach was protected from poachers, their numbers started inching upwards toward sustainability. Another success factor is that newly laid eggs collected in Mexico have been transplanted on other beaches in the Gulf. Mature females are now returning to nest at their new natal beaches. The heartbreak turtle will survive.

Like all other sea turtles, a Kemp's female lays several clutches of eggs during the nesting season. After covering her nest and tamping the sand down with a curious dancing, hopping movement she returns to the sea to rest for three or four weeks and then comes back ashore. After laying her third clutch of eggs, she heads back to her feeding grounds. In a couple of years she will return to do it all over again. The cycle will continue for the rest of her life.

The eggs that a turtle lays are the future of the species. Making it back to the natal beach and laying those precious eggs has fulfilled her destiny, a destiny that began as a little hatchling scampering across wet sand many years before. In a couple of months the new babies will start their own great journey. Those eggs are the most precious thing that a turtle ever has or creates and she gives them up so that new turtles will have their chance to do the same.

A NEW PART of us is always trying to be born. In the cycle of life, we go out into the world to work or study or raise a family or travel. We leave nests and follow our compass. We discover our gifts and look for the place where those talents have the most impact. We sink to our depths during difficult times and search for meaning in that place. Then, suddenly, we have the experience of coming home. We arrive at the inner destination. We get there because something has been growing inside of us, a new belief in ourselves, some wisdom, a precious egg of knowledge or discovery.

Shortly after our time in the Sahara I was in Korea to give a speech to several thousand insurance agents. The timing was perfect because I was able to watch myself costarring in Young Joong's film on the Korean Broadcasting System. Even better, I had the chance to see Young Joong again.

I was delighted to see Young Joong and I told him that I was very proud of him for the beautiful film he had made in the Sahara. He looked more grown up, stronger and more confident than he was in the desert and I could tell that he had come back to Korea to his own inner homecoming. The Sahara was the outer journey to help him find that inner treasure – that he could be a good father, a good husband and a good filmmaker all at the same time.

I received an e-mail about two months later from Young Joong. He was making a documentary in the Himalayas. He had climbed easily to an altitude of 13,500 feet, the base camp of Annapurna, to film the record breaking ascent of Oh Eun-sun, one of the world's best female mountaineers. I thought back to his struggle climbing just a 1,000-foot sand dune and smiled, knowing that eggs laid in the desert were now hatching in the snow of the Himalayas.

Young Joong vowed that he would return to the Sahara within five years. Perhaps he will find more of himself when he goes back. I couldn't wait that long. One year later I went back again with Virginie Biarnay, the same wonderful Tuareg guides and other intrepid travelers. But these are just outer journeys that mirror what we are doing inside. No matter how often I or Young Joong return to the Sahara, we will always have to leave at some point. Even the inner homecoming, the arrival of our destiny, doesn't last forever. We must leave that experience too. But having named and claimed the fruits of our journey, the essential truth of who we are, we've gained a stronger connection with our deepest core, and carry that with us as newly born hatchings on our next journey to the sea.

This is the endless and eternal cycle of turtles and of people: coming and going, departing and returning. Our journeys can last a minute, a day, six months or 33 years. But however long we are out there at sea, all that matters is that we find and follow our compass. Because it will always bring us home to ourselves, our destiny and the life we were meant to live.

EPILOGUE

Australia is home to the flatback turtle, the least studied, least understood and most mysterious species of sea turtle. It is about the size of the hawksbill, and can weigh up to 200 pounds. It nests exclusively on remote Australian beaches and lays the smallest clutches of all sea turtles, about 50 eggs. But the flatback's eggs are much bigger, almost the size of leatherback eggs. So too are the hatchlings oversized.

Flatbacks are the only species that does not venture into open ocean immediately upon leaving the nest. In fact, this turtle never goes into the deep ocean waters at any stage of life. The flatback is a bit of a homebody but it must still forage for food. While making sure that it never leaves the Australian continental shelf, the flatback often travels hundreds of miles to feeding grounds after nesting. It still has a life similarly nomadic to the other six species and like the others, it literally carries its home on its back.

🐢

LIKE A TURTLE'S SHELL, your deepest self, your compass and your destiny protect and house you. Whenever you leave a nest in life, everything that matters comes right along with you, including your inner home. You too can be at home wherever you are. Let this image of the turtle's shell, and the security it provides, be the inspiration for your own epic voyage, as you follow the great magnetic pull of the life you were meant to live.

Flatback sea turtle (Natator depressus)

Australia is also home to the latest addition to our family, my grandson Nash. I'm very at home as a grandfather and pursue this compass heading with joy and delight. I look forward to watching this little turtle scamper toward the sea, most likely with a tiny surfboard in his arm.

As I write these final thoughts I am not far from my daughter and grandson and the habitat of the flatback turtle. I am in Queenstown, New Zealand. I was told that I would feel very at home here. The South Island's snow-capped mountains and deep fjord-like lakes remind many of British Columbia. But something is wrong and I feel like tucking my head into my turtle shell for safety.

I've just woken up in my hotel room and I'm confused. It's dark and my bed is shaking. I'm jet-lagged from having crossed so many time zones to get here from Canada. I look at my watch. It's 4:35 in the morning. I still can't understand why my bed is shaking.

As my head clears I wonder if I've checked into a honeymoon hotel and the couple in the room next door are simply doing what newlyweds do. Then I notice the coat hangers in the closet on the opposite wall are clanging around to the same rhythm that is shaking my bed. I am in the middle of a powerful earthquake. After a very long minute the shaking stops and I call downstairs to the front desk. The clerk confirms that this was indeed an earthquake but there does not seem to be any damage to the hotel.

I sleep fitfully for another few hours. When I wake up and head down to the hotel restaurant for breakfast, I discover that a very large 7.1-magnitude earthquake has struck Christchurch, just 300 miles from where I am. 100,000 homes have been damaged, very few people have water service or electricity. Bridges are down, streets are cracked and impassable and everyone is afraid of big aftershocks causing more damage and danger. Miraculously, no one has died.

New Zealand is in one of the most active earthquake zones on Earth. So is the West Coast of North America, where I live. Vancouver Island experiences a cataclysmic earthquake every 300 years or so. They tell us that "the Big One" could happen any time. There is nothing like getting a "wake-up call" such as I did in Queenstown to remember how powerful this hidden force at the core of our planet really is. Earthquakes remind us that our planet is far from the solid, immovable object that we think it is.

You, and I, and the Earth, are in a constant process of growth. Sometimes the change is subtle and deep and goes unnoticed. Other times it is a tectonic shift that upsets us from our core right to the surface of our daily lives. The energy at the core of the Earth and the power deep inside us are both very big forces to reckon with. The advantage we have is that our compass is picking up signals from our core all the time. Thanks to the attractions we feel, the talents and abilities we possess, the mistakes that we make and the depths that we dive to, we are able to find our way out into the world and then find our way home, over and over again, so that ultimately, we are always at home wherever we are.

AFTERWORD

SAVING THE SEA TURTLES

Magnificent sea turtles are in peril. Some species are more threatened than others. But we will almost certainly see the extinction of the Pacific leatherback in the near future without quick and significant changes to protect them.

Scientists estimate that only one percent of the total number of sea turtles that existed at the beginning of the 20th century currently inhabit the world's oceans. The greatest threats to their survival are industrial fishing, local harvesting of turtles for food, development on nesting sites and egg poaching.

There are many organizations devoted to saving sea turtles and any of them would welcome your support. But there are also some very important things individuals can do to help ensure the survival of these elegant animals who inspire us with their epic journeys.

The most important thing is ensuring that governments enact and enforce turtle-friendly fishing regulations. Even if you do not live in a country where turtles feed or nest, international deep sea fishing fleets may accidentally be harming or killing thousands of turtles each year through unintentionally catching them in nets or on long-line hooks.

Contact your government agency that regulates fishing to find out if there is a need for better rules concerning turtle safety at sea. You can also encourage your government to adopt and enforce international treaties that are already in place to protect turtles.

Before you consume seafood, ask if it was caught using turtle-friendly methods, especially if you are dining on shrimp.

One of the best and certainly most enjoyable things to do is visit or vacation in countries where turtles nest and feed. Explore the beaches and swim in the waters. If you are lucky enough to observe a turtle laying its eggs or a nest hatching or even see one swimming alone along a coral reef, you will want to protect them more than ever. Let the local people know that you are there because of the turtles.

It is estimated that a single, live hawksbill is worth $30,000 to the local economy near its feeding or nesting grounds. Encourage the locals to care for this natural living resource. This will help reduce egg poaching, live harvesting of turtles for food and beachfront development where turtles nest.

It is not too late. Together, we can make a difference and guarantee the ongoing survival of these beautiful, ancient and inspiring creatures of the sea.

ALSO BY STEVE DONAHUE

The gripping story of Steve Donahue's odyssey across the Sahara Desert is a metaphor for transitional times in our lives. Unlike mountains, with their clear routes and identifiable peaks, much of life more closely resembles a desert. We get lost, we get stuck, we chase mirages and the journey seems endless. Donahue skillfully weaves the true tale of his harrowing adventure with "Six Rules of Desert Travel" that will help you gracefully cross all of your personal deserts.

Published by Berrett-Koehler Publishers, Inc., Paperback $16.95

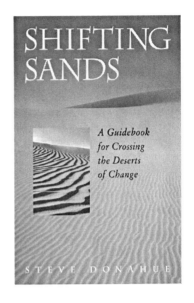

"*Shifting Sands* is a thoroughly engaging and enjoyable read that is certain to shift your outlook on life. Steve Donahue's stories and lessons capture the human condition in a deeply profound way and will captivate and enrich anyone who picks this book up."

- David Irvine, author of *Simple Living in a Complex World* and *Becoming Real: Journey to Authenticity*

"Tired of goal-setting and goal-getting? Soulful yet practical, *Shifting Sands* is required reading when your clear mountain peak becomes a long, lonely desert of change."

- Jennifer Lawler, martial arts coach and author of *Dojo Wisdom: 100 Simple Ways to Become a Stronger, Calmer, More Courageous Person*

CPSIA information can be obtained
at www.ICGtesting.com
Printed in the USA
FFOW03n0530091217
43963409-43090FF